How to grow your dinner without leaving the house.

Claire Ratinon

How to grow your dinner without leaving the house.

Laurence King Publishing

LAURENCE KING

Published by Laurence King Publishing Ltd
361-373 City Road
London EC1V 1LR
Tel: +44 (0)20 7841 6900
Email: enquiries@laurenceking.com
www.laurenceking.com

A catalog record for this book is
available from the British Library.

ISBN: 978-1-78627-737-4

Commissioning editor: Zara Larcombe
Photography: Ida Riveros, Rita Platts, and
    Claire Ratinon
Design: Masumi Briozzo

Printed in China

A Note on Plant Varieties:
We have included a range of varieties within our
Plant Profiles, but not all of these will be available
worldwide. However, the principles discussed in
each profile will still apply and allow you to grow
happy and healthy produce.

Laurence King Publishing is committed to
ethical and sustainable production. We are
proud participants in The Book Chain Project®
bookchainproject.com

Contents

Why grow your own food?

As an urban dweller who discovered her love of plants while living in a one-bedroom apartment with no outside space at all, I'm familiar with the overwhelming urge to grow vegetables without a garden. My journey from documentary filmmaker to urban food-grower has seen me growing plants wherever I could find the opportunity: from raised beds in East London elementary schools to a summer spent taking care of thousands of potted plants on a disused parking lot, and from installing pollinator-friendly planters in subway stations to growing organic salad on a tiny site in Hackney. When you're determined to grow plants in a city, you make it happen wherever you can!

I honestly believe that if you want to grow your own, it is possible. Even in the city, even without a garden, even if your outside space is tiny and paved over. You might not achieve self-sufficiency, but you can experience the pleasure of nurturing a seed into a plant that ends up on your plate. It is a simple but humbling process. It's not always easy, but it needn't be too difficult if you're up for learning how to give a plant what it needs to survive, and thrive, in a pot.

Growing plants has led me to more than just delicious fresh produce. It has been a gateway to better mental and physical health. It has allowed me to access a deep gratitude for all those who have a role in growing our food, and it has enabled me to connect with the natural world that supports us and with the seasons through which we move every year. Most importantly, it has prompted me to cultivate an ever-expanding awareness of the systems that feed us, and to do my best to tread as lightly on our extraordinary Earth as I can. That is why I grow my plants following organic principles, an approach that respects and honours the many natural systems that make it possible for plants to grow for our benefit and nourishment.

My sincerest hope is that, through this book, you'll feel encouraged to explore the joy of growing vegetables for your dinner and all the other wonderful things that adventuring with plants can bring.

GETTING STARTED

The basics

Understanding what a plant needs in order to flourish is vital if you want to grow your own. Edible plants need more of your attention and awareness than houseplants if they are to produce deliciousness for your plate.

Light

There's no green plant that can live without the light of the sun. Photosynthesis is the process whereby a plant takes sunlight, carbon dioxide, and water and turns them into energy to grow. This magical process is foundational for the existence of all living things.

Water

Water is necessary for photosynthesis, for moving minerals, nutrients, and food around the plant, and for enabling the plant to stand upright. Although all plants need water, it's worth noting that all have different needs, and too much can be as bad as too little.

Temperature

Plants, like all other living things, respond to the temperature of their environment and— as is the case with light and water—different plants need different conditions to thrive. Each plant has an optimal soil temperature for germination, an ideal temperature for growth, and a minimum temperature for flowering, fruiting, and ripening.

Growing medium

All the plants that you'll be growing to eat need something to grow in, and, since in this book we're not talking about growing in garden soil, that's going to be compost. The growing medium is essential for holding the water and nutrients a plant needs to absorb through its roots, for having the right structure for roots to anchor into for stability, and for holding pockets of air so the roots can breathe.

Pollination

If the edible part of the plant you're growing is a fruit, its flower will need to be pollinated to transform it into that fruit. Different plants have evolved alongside their ideal pollinator— whether bees, butterflies, beetles or wind— but in their absence, it is possible for us to intervene to ensure that our plants produce a bountiful crop.

VIOLA TRICOLOR
"VIOLA"

Annual vs perennial

I remember how confusing I found these two words when I started learning about plants, but it's really useful to get your head around them. Annual plants have a life cycle that goes from seed to harvest in less than a year (sometimes only a month or two). Perennials, on the other hand, can live for several years because they have the physical makeup to survive through all seasons—even if they "hibernate" or die back in the winter, they will start to grow again when the weather warms up. Most of the plants in this book are grown as annuals, so it's probably not worth trying to nurse them through the winter in the hope they'll grow again the following year (although I have known people to do this!), because they will be very, very sad.

Life in a pot

Growing plants in containers makes it possible to grow your own produce in the smallest of spaces, and the main role of a container gardener is to understand what a plant requires to thrive. When it comes to water, food, room to grow, and a spot with just the right amount of light, your potted plants will rely on you entirely to meet their needs.

The best part of container growing is how much control you have: you can repot your plants if they need more or new soil, you can find a new location if they need more sunshine, and you can place them out of the reach of common garden pests such as slugs and snails. Container plants need less weeding, are easier to feed, and can fit into all kinds of spaces.

Understanding your space

Before you start on your growing journey, you need to spend a little time assessing the space you have available for your plants. You'll need to figure out the following:

· How much space do you have for containers?
· What direction does your growing space face? (The ideal is south-facing, as it gets the most sunlight hours, but east and west can work too)
· Is the sun obstructed for part of the day? (Generally, leafy plants can tolerate some shade, but plants that produce fruit need 6-8 hours of sunlight per day.)
· If you're growing on a balcony, is there a weight limit? A 10-gallon pot full of recently watered soil is pretty heavy.
· How exposed to the wind is your growing space?
· Do you have somewhere to put a hanging basket?
· Do you have a sturdy fence or a wall that you can grow climbing plants up or fix small containers to?

Deciding what to grow

One of the most exciting parts of growing plants for your dinner is deciding what to grow! The best way to do that is to ask yourself what you like to eat. There's really no point putting in all the energy and effort required to raise a happy, healthy zucchini plant if you don't like them—particularly since a single zucchini plant can produce up to 30 fruits!

After answering that question, consider the following:

· What vegetables do you like to eat or want to try that are not easy to find in the store? Spicy mustard leaves, oddly shaped or coloured potatoes, white-skinned eggplants, dark chocolate-coloured chili peppers?

· What produce is most expensive and what would be worth growing yourself? Grocery store herbs can be particularly costly, when you think about how much of them you use. Growing your own means you can harvest just before you cook, which is fresher, healthier, more delicious and much more cost-effective.

· How much time do you have to spend on your plants? If you're pressed for time, you might want to steer away from plants that need lots of watering and feeding to thrive, such as tomatoes and peppers.

· Is there a vegetable you love that you'd like to try a different variety of? The majority of the world's food comes from only 30 different types of plant, so even if you eat a great range of produce, you're still limited to the handful of varieties that are available in the store. Growing your own allows you to try the many wild and wonderful varieties of your favourite vegetables and discover how exquisite they can taste.

Planning your growing space

Now that you've had some ideas about what you'd like to grow and have got a sense of the potential of your growing space, you can start to plan. Measure the area you're planning to fill with plants and determine how many pots you can comfortably fit into it.

You'll want to use pots that give your plants enough space to grow to their full size, so to some extent this exercise will also help you decide what you can grow. Opposite there are two diagrams showing how much you could cram onto two different sized balconies:

Balcony 1
· One zucchini plant in a 10-gallon container
· One early potato plant in an 8-gallon growbag
· Two dwarf tomato plants, each in 6-gallon growbags
· Two 0.8-gallon pots of pea plants (two plants per pot)
· Two 1-gallon pots of beets
· Four 0.4-gallon pots of radishes
· Six 4in pots of salad leaves
· Four 0.2-gallon pots of herbs
· One wormery

Balcony 2
· One large window box of hanging tomatoes and basil
· One early potato plant in a 8-gallon growbag
· Two small window boxes of hanging nasturtiums, violets, and chives
· Three 4in pots of salad leaves

· One 1-gallon pot of dwarf French beans
· One 0.4-gallon pot of rosemary, thyme, or oregano
· Two 0.2-gallon pot of radishes, parsley, and cilantro

Put the sun-loving fruiting plants (such as tomatoes, peppers, and eggplants) in a spot that gets good sunlight and salad leaves in areas that are a little shadier. If there's a corner that's too dark to grow anything in, you could set up a wormery (see page 50).

If you're using a balcony that gets a little windy, consider putting up a windbreak to provide shelter and protect your plants from damage or drying out too quickly. And if there's a balcony below yours, it might be worth checking where the water that drains from your pots goes, to avoid any arguments with the neighbors.

If you've got limited space, it's not very wise to devote a large section to a big vegetable such as zucchini. Unless you're hopelessly infatuated with a special variety that is impossible to buy in the store, I would suggest choosing smaller, quicker crops that make the most of your space

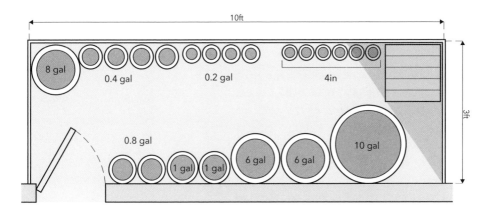

Balcony 1

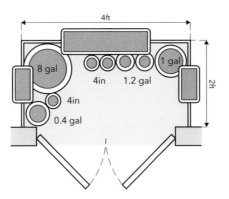

Balcony 2

Planning your season

The final piece of the organizational puzzle is planning your season. One of the most important lessons this part of the process teaches us is that edible plants do best during their specific growing season. Despite the illusion the grocery stores create of year-round supplies of all fruits and vegetables, each edible plant actually has an optimal time of year to grow through its life cycle, from seed to harvest.

So, you've decided what you want to grow and you've determined that you've got space for it. Now you can create a calendar of your main gardening activities. If you work this out in advance you can ensure that you've got the seeds, pots, equipment, compost, and time you need to get growing.

Keeping a growing diary

Whenever I'm asked what single piece of advice I'd give to budding container gardeners, I always say: "Keep a diary, keep notes on everything–your future gardening self will thank you if you write it all down!"

Your growing diary doesn't need to be fancy, but it should have enough space for you to record your actions and observations as you move through the growing season. Not only is note-taking useful for showing your plants' progress and helping you learn how they change, but also it's an opportunity to observe how they react to your intervention and the conditions around them, and to spot patterns from year to year.

In my growing diary, I keep notes on:
· The weather and highest and lowest temperatures (especially when it falls below freezing)
· Dates of seed-sowing, transplanting, and planting out
· Observations on the development of my plants
· Feeding and fertilizing
· A plant's changing watering needs
· Signs of problems–pests, diseases, nutrient deficiencies–and how I addressed them (see pages 48-9 for more information)

- Unexpected events—e.g., suspected squirrel attack
- Harvest records—dates and yield
- Anything that deviates from my plans for the season.

By keeping clear and detailed notes, you can learn what works and what doesn't, and how your actions are key to whether your edible plants survive and thrive. Ultimately, observation and note-taking are a gateway to staying connected to the entire growing process—and that is the key to growing plants successfully.

Tools and materials

Seed compost

The medium you sow your seeds into is different from the soil in gardens and the compost you fill pots with. It should be low in nutrients, hold water without becoming saturated and ideally be free of pests, soil diseases, and weed seeds. It should also feel light and fluffy; if it is dense and full of clumps, it will benefit from being broken up and mixed with vermiculite (see below).

Multipurpose compost

Move on to using this kind of compost when potting on your seedlings and filling containers. It's the ideal composition for the plants you'll be growing—and fortunately organic ones are available. I prefer to use peat-free multipurpose compost because it is more environmentally friendly.

Vermiculite

Vermiculite is a natural mineral that can be added to compost to increase its capacity to retain moisture and nutrients. It can also help to aerate the soil, which is essential for root development and health.

Seed trays

You can sow seeds in any shallow container with drainage holes, but I do like to use modular seed trays: they make it possible to sow different varieties in one tray, because they keep the seedlings separate. This is definitely what you need in a small space.

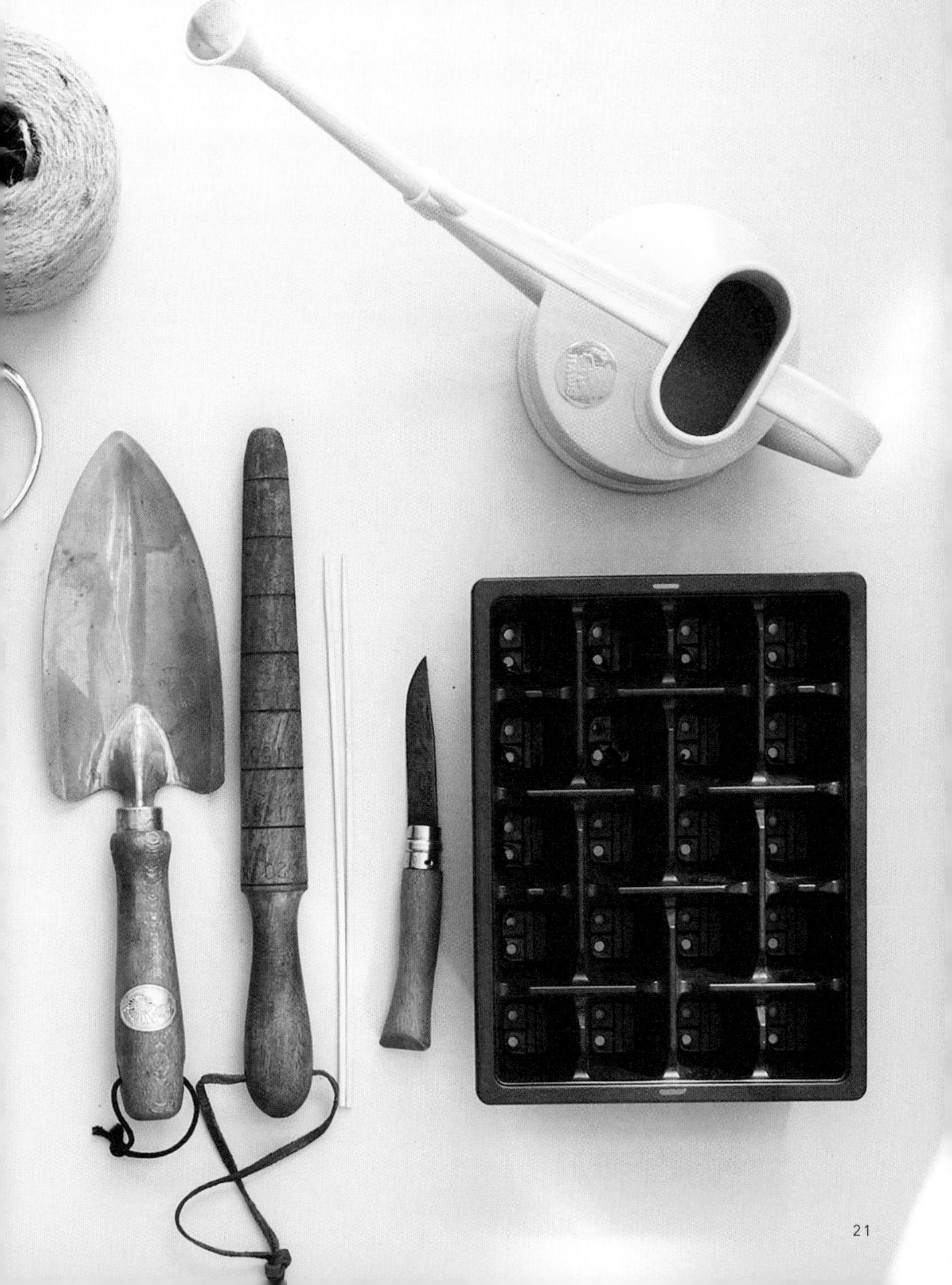

Labels

Labels are non-negotiable! You can make them by cutting up yogurt pots, use wooden coffee stirrers, or buy the purpose-made kind. I prefer to recycle, but if I do buy some, I get the wooden kind because, although they don't last as long, they're not adding more plastic to a world that already has too much.

Trowel

This isn't essential for all container gardeners, especially if you're growing small crops in small pots, but it's worth having one nearby when you're handling larger plants. It's easier to fill your pots with compost and to dig a hole for planting out with a tool that is designed for the job. Alternatively, you can just use your hands.

Dibber

A dibber is essentially a small stick that you use to make holes in the compost where you'll sow your seed. It is not essential to have a "real" dibber for small-space growing though, as you can improvise with various household objects such as chopsticks, an old pen or, if the seed is big enough, the tip of your finger.

Watering can (with a rose)

Watering is done differently at different stages of the growing process. A small watering can with a rose (which is the word for the piece that attaches to the spout) with tiny holes allows you to water your seed compost evenly without saturating it or washing it away. (You can make your own by poking tiny holes in the lid of a water bottle.) If you're mostly growing in small pots, you'll need a small watering can with a thin spout to have control over the amount and direction of the water. Larger plants, such as zucchinis, tomatoes, and potatoes, are thirsty, so it's worth having a larger can if you're planning to grow those.

Heated propagator

A propagator is a worthwhile investment, especially if you want to grow cold-sensitive plants such as tomatoes, basil, and chilies. Effectively a mini-greenhouse, a propagator is designed to give your seedlings a warm and protected start, and is often deployed when the days are still dark and the weather cold. By warming the soil and trapping that warmth and moisture under a clear cover, seeds can be germinated and start growing earlier in the season than those that are started without.

Grow light

Although they are a bit pricey, grow lights are useful for starting seeds early in a propagator, and essential for anyone with no outdoor space and low light levels. They are designed to emit light that has exactly the same range of wavelengths as the sun's rays, so that the plants can photosynthesize. A grow light on top of a heated propagator is the ideal setup for your little seedlings to get started in early spring.

Scissors, snips, or a harvest knife

It is useful to have a sharp blade on hand for harvesting and for pruning shoots and leaves. Ensuring that you make clean cuts when removing parts of your plants is essential to keep them healthy.

Twine

This is really handy for tying your plants to support structures or canes. I prefer to use twine made of jute as it is a natural material that rarely causes damage to growing stems and branches. It's also biodegradable and so better for the environment than plastic twine.

SOWING SEEDS AND RAISING PLANTS

How to sow seeds

Seed-sowing—the very beginning of the growing journey—is a simple but wonderful process, and one of my favorite tasks. Although it's straightforward, it must be executed well if your plants are to have the best start in life.

When planting seeds, you are creating the conditions that send a message to the seed that it's time to germinate and start transforming into a plant. Generally speaking, that means adding water, changing the temperature, and providing something for the plant to grow in.

Seed-sowing compost is different from the kind that is used elsewhere. It has a light, fine texture and is low in nutrients, since all the food a plant needs to get started is within the seed itself, and, in fact, the delicate seed can be scorched if there are too many nutrients in the compost. If your seed compost seems dense, you can add some vermiculite to create a lighter, airier mix. A helpful rule of thumb is that a seed should be planted at a depth equal to double its diameter. For example, if a pea seed is ¼in wide, you'll need to bury it ½in under the surface of the compost.

1 Fill the pot, seed tray, or module tray (make sure there are drainage holes) with compost to the top, and use another pot or tray to compress it, gently but firmly.

2 Water the compost well and allow the excess water to drain away. (Seeds that are watered after you've sown them can sometimes be displaced or washed away.)

3 Place small seeds evenly across the surface of the compost or in each module. When sowing larger seeds, use a dibber, chopstick, or finger to create a good-sized hole to place the seed in. Don't overcrowd the seeds: seedlings really appreciate having room to grow.

4 Sprinkle a layer of compost over the seeds.

5 Gently press the compost down onto the seeds to ensure they make contact with it.

6 Write a label for the seeds, including the variety name and the date of sowing. This is really important, because most newly emerged seedlings look exactly the same.

7 Either cover the pots with a clear plastic bag or cover the tray with a clear lid. This will create a moist and warm environment that will help the seeds to germinate.

8 Place the pots or modules in a tray that has no drainage holes, so that you can water from below as your seedlings grow—this method encourages the plant's roots to grow downwards. Don't let the compost dry out completely or become saturated with water.

9 Some seeds—such as tomatoes, chilies, peppers, and basil—prefer to germinate in warm soil, so place their trays somewhere warm or in a heated propagator, if you have one.

10 Once the seedlings begin to emerge, take the bag or lid off your seed tray so your seedlings don't get too moist or even moldy.

Some seeds require additional steps. For the plants covered in this book, these steps are included in their individual profiles.

How to raise strong seedlings

When your seedlings first emerge they are pretty fragile, so treat them gently. If you care for them by following these instructions, they'll grow up to be strong, have a better chance of resisting diseases and pests, and reach maturity to provide you with a harvest.

Water

Watering very young seedlings from above can damage or dislodge them as they're trying to establish themselves, so I prefer to water from below (into the outer tray, so the soil absorbs what it can). This encourages strong root development, because the seedlings reach downwards to seek out water. Be very careful not to overwater, since soggy soil can cause tender young roots to rot–give the soil time to absorb what it needs (say 20 minutes) then pour away any that is left in the outer tray.

Light

As soon as your seedlings' first leaves unfurl, you need to think about light. If you don't have a bright windowsill or bay window to put them in, they'll need to go under a grow light for up to 12 hours a day so they get the light they need to photosynthesize and grow. Plants grow toward the light, so if you are keeping your seedlings on a windowsill, it is vitally important to turn them either 90 or 180 degrees at least once a day. This will ensure that they grow evenly and don't stretch toward the light, becoming what gardeners call "leggy," meaning tall, scrawny, and feeble–not the qualities you're trying to cultivate in your young plants!

Touch

When young plants grow outdoors, they have to cope with the elements, which encourages them to grow up sturdy and robust. Seedlings grown indoors are far more coddled, and this can lead them to become weak plants. You can address this by gently stroking your seedlings regularly to mimic the buffeting of rain and wind. Alternatively, you can set a fan to blow gently on them for an hour or so every day. Plus, the improved air circulation can help prevent disease.

Transplanting

Some edible plants–radishes, microgreens and potatoes, for example–live in the same container for their whole life; others, such as lettuce and annual herbs, can be transplanted while relatively small into their final location. Larger vegetable plants, such as tomatoes, chilies and bell peppers, spend some of their early life in an intermediary container before being planted in their grown-up pot. This gives them more space to grow, while keeping them protected until they're big and strong enough to face the outside world.

Once the seedlings to be transplanted have one or two sets of "true leaves" (those that grow after the first pair of seed leaves), you can upgrade them to a 3in pot as follows:

1 Water the seedlings thoroughly. Fill a 3in pot with multipurpose compost using the same approach of compressing and watering as when sowing seed.

2 Using a teaspoon, lift the seedling from beneath the roots, being careful to cause as little damage as possible. Make a hole in the compost that's the same depth as your seedling's root ball and place the plant carefully in, holding it by the leaves, not the stem.

3 Fill in the hole with compost and gently firm the seedling in.

4 Top the soil with a thin layer of vermiculite to help prevent "damping off," a fungal disease that dwells in wet soil and can cause your vulnerable young plants to rot and die. Transplanting can be quite a shocking process for a plant. It's best done in the evening or on a cloudy day so the plant has time to recover from the move before getting on with photosynthesizing at full capacity.

If after a few weeks your plants are drying out quickly after watering or their roots appear to be filling the 3in pot, if growth has slowed down, or, worse, if the leaves are curling or discolored (a sign the compost is low in nutrients) but it's too soon to move your seedlings outside, you might consider repotting again, one size up.

MOVING SEEDLINGS INTO CONTAINERS

Choosing containers for your plants

Pretty much anything can be converted into a container for your edible plants. I've seen plants growing in old shoes, bathtubs, tires, reusable shopping bags, strainers, and even a disused toilet! As long as the vessel provides enough room for the soil a plant needs and for its root system, has drainage holes, and is sturdy enough to support the plant as it gets bigger, you can use anything.

Capacity

Choose a container with the capacity to hold your plant when it is fully grown. Each plant requires a minimum capacity (see Plant Profiles, pages 55–112) to thrive, and it's important to give them enough room or you may run into problems with watering and feeding. For example, big plants such as zucchinis need at least 7 gallons of compost to grow healthily, whereas shallow-rooting plants such as lettuce can grow in a container as little as 3in deep.

Drainage

Providing the right amount of water for your plants is something of an art, and making sure your containers have adequate drainage is an essential part of that process. Although your plants need water to survive and flourish, too much can be fatal. Drainage holes allow excess water to drain out of the container so the compost doesn't become saturated and the plants' roots don't suffocate, rot, and die.

Material

Different materials have different qualities and drawbacks. Plastic pots are light and good at retaining moisture but, although reusable, are not usually recyclable. Terra-cotta and clay pots are sturdier but heavier (good if your growing space is a bit windy); since they are porous, the compost inside them dries out quickly, so they're great for a drought-tolerant rosemary but not for thirsty plants. Metal containers are durable but can warm up quickly in full sun, so wouldn't be suitable for lettuces, which are liable to wilt in the heat. Wooden planters are handsome, sturdy, and easy to build (or buy), but they can rot over time, so lining them with a semi-permeable material (or some thick plastic with draining holes poked through it) will make them last longer.

Also, if you're recycling or upcycling containers that weren't originally intended for growing plants, it's important to consider what they are made from. Tires, for example, have been said to leach chemicals when exposed repeatedly to water. Try to avoid anything that might compromise the health of your plants, given that you're going to be eating the fruit and vegetables they produce.

Weight

Once your containers are filled with compost and plants, and watered, they can get pretty heavy. If you're growing in a space that has a weight limit (such as a balcony or roof terrace), or if the container will be hung from a bracket or hook, you must choose lightweight containers—this will also save your back from the strain of lugging heavy pots around. For bigger plants, choose a position and commit to it before planting up—a watered potato plant in a hefty growbag will be nearly impossible to move!

I currently grow my plants in plastic pots because they're easy to find second-hand and simple to use and reuse, and are both light and water-retentive—and it saves them from ending up in landfill. And if you don't love the look of them, you can always pop them inside a container that's more visually appealing.

Choosing compost for your plants

Unlike growing in a garden, where you already have soil to work with, container gardening requires you to choose—and sometimes create—the medium for your plants to grow in. This can be a challenge to get right, but it's also an amazing opportunity to have some control over an essential aspect of growing. It can help you avoid the problems that come with growing in garden soil, such as soil-borne diseases and pests.

Garden soil is simply too heavy to use in containers, so we turn to compost to fill our pots. The word "compost" is used interchangeably in the gardening world to refer both to the stuff you buy in bags from the garden center and to the sweetly earthy garden compost produced from decomposing fruit and vegetable scraps in a compost heap. Although garden compost is very nutritious (and is useful if you can get your hands on some), I will be talking about the bagged kind, because this works best in containers. A wide range of bagged growing mediums is available from garden centers, ranging from topsoil to well-rotted manure, but ideally what you want is peat-free multipurpose compost.

The main functions of a growing medium are to provide something for the plant to root down into, and to allow it to get exactly the right amount of water and nutrients. Multipurpose compost has the right weight and structure to hold water and air around the roots while allowing the excess to drain away, and contains between four and six weeks' nutrients.

When preparing compost for planting, I tip it into a container and break up any lumps, then mix in a generous scoop of vermiculite and a sprinkling of organic seaweed meal, which will act as a slow-release all-round fertilizer, supplementing the limited nutrients already in the compost. You could also add a handful of garden compost for added nutritional benefit if you have a generous family member, friend, or community garden with a healthy compost heap and enough to spare.

Putting your plants in containers

For the plants that will have to spend their adult life outside–in hanging baskets, on doorsteps, on verandas or on balconies–you have to decide when to move them from indoors into their main containers. Any big change is a shock for a plant, and the move from inside to outside is the biggest transition they'll go through. To prepare them, we put them through the process of "hardening off."

Hardening off

This term describes the gradual exposure of a plant to conditions outside. It gives the plant the opportunity to acclimatize as much as possible to full sunshine and temperature fluctuations before being permanently moved into its grown-up container.

It can be done by placing the plant outside in partial shade during the day and bringing it back inside before the temperature drops at night. Do this for 7–14 days, steadily increasing the plant's exposure to the sun.

The plants in this book that are grown and looked after this way are sensitive to temperatures below freezing, so start this process only when the threat of frost has passed. That's when you can leave your plant out at night without it freezing to death!

Planting out

Once your plants have been hardened off, they're ready to be planted into their final containers.

1 Water the young plant a few hours before transplanting.

2 Fill a container (the correct capacity for the fully grown plant) three-quarters full with your compost mix, make a hole big enough to accommodate the current pot, and water generously.

3 Release the plant from its pot by placing your hand over the top, with the stem between your fingers, tipping it over into your palm and pulling the pot off. Gently loosen the roots– especially if they've started to grow into a pot shape–and carefully place the plant into its new container.

4 Add more compost to cover all the roots and firm the plant in. Water in if you think the compost isn't moist enough.

Most plants prefer to be planted no deeper than they were in their original container, apart from tomatoes, which benefit from being buried to just below their first leaves; each of the tiny hairs on the stem will then transform into a root.

Keep your newly transplanted plants well watered over the next few days, and don't worry if they look a bit sad to start with—they'll perk up once they've got over the stress of being moved.

TAKING CARE OF YOUR PLANTS

Watering plants in containers

Giving the plants the water they need is one of the container gardener's main jobs, and providing the wrong amount can lead to slowed growth, wilting, rotting, early seed production (bolting), and nutrient deficiency. The amount of water a plant requires depends on the plant itself, the type and size of container, and the weather. The more diligently you observe your plants, the better you'll become at understanding their watering needs.

One of the virtues of multipurpose compost is that it's designed to hold on to the water a plant needs while allowing any excess to drain away (so don't forget to place the pot on a tray or plate or in an area that won't be bothered by some runoff). Nonetheless, since the plants are limited to the pot, they can't grow an extensive root system to find the water they need, so it's down to you to provide it.

Here are some general principles:

· Most of the plants in this book require generous amounts of water when they're actively growing, and prefer not to dry out completely between waterings.
· Test the moisture level by sticking your finger down into the compost. Sometimes the top of the soil might be dry but the bottom isn't, so you could hold off watering for the time being.

· Water your plants in the morning or evening, when the temperature is lower and there is no direct sun, to prevent water loss through evaporation.
· A thorough drenching is better than little and often, because it ensures that all the plant's roots have access to water. Shallow watering can lead to roots growing only near the surface of the soil, where they're more vulnerable.
· Water the soil, not the leaves. You're aiming for the roots.
· Use room-temperature water; water cold from the faucet can be shocking for roots, especially if the plant is still young. I like to fill my watering can after I've used it so that it's full of tepid water the next time I need it.
· Make sure your containers aren't sitting in water—most edible plants don't like having wet feet.

Monitor the weather. When it's hot, some of your plants will need watering twice a day.

If the soil has become so dry that the water runs straight through it, immerse the entire pot in a bucket of water until it has rehydrated.

· If you have the space for a small water butt, collecting rainwater is a great way to conserve water.

Feeding your plants

One of the limitations of container growing is that once the nutrients and minerals in the compost have run out, you must supplement them if your plants are to keep growing, flowering, and fruiting.

The main nutrients that plants absorb from their growing medium are:

· Nitrogen, which is needed for leaf and shoot growth; it is part of every protein in a plant
· Phosphorus, which is required for the growth of roots, cell division, and new tissue development
· Potassium, which is needed for flowering and fruiting.

Plants also need micronutrients, including calcium, magnesium, iron, and boron.

A range of fertilizers is available, and many are the chemical kind that may do the job but are terrible for the environment. I prefer to use organic or homemade options when I can to feed my hungry plants:

Garden compost
If you can get hold of good-quality garden compost, it is a valuable source of all the nutrients a plant needs. You can either incorporate it into your multipurpose compost when planting out, or soak some in water to create a compost "tea" that you can dilute and use as feed for your plants.

Worm compost
If you have a productive wormery, the worm casts (poop!) that it produces are rich in nutrients; the worms also produce a liquid that can be diluted and used to feed your plants.

Nettle tea
This nitrogen-rich liquid feed, ideal for leafy plants such as lettuce and chard, can be made from stinging nettles steeped in water. Fill a container (preferably one with a lid) with nettles and weigh the leaves down with a stone, then cover with water. Leave for a couple of weeks, by which point it will stink, but that just means it's working! Dilute the brown liquid until it is the colour of weak tea and feed your adult plants with it.

Comfrey tea
Comfrey is an amazing plant with a very long taproot that brings precious nutrients up from the depths of the soil and into its leaves, and you can use it to produce a tea, as with nettles above. It can take about a month to become usable, but it's worth the wait because it's rich in potassium and can be used on all your fruiting plants, such as tomatoes and zucchinis.

Seaweed fertilizer

This is an excellent all-rounder, but since I don't live near the sea this is one I've never made. It is a bit pricey, but it does such a good job of providing a range of nutrients that it's worth it. Use seaweed meal to enrich your growing medium or liquid seaweed fertilizer as a regular feed for hungry plants such as potatoes.

Finally, don't be tempted to fertilize too often. This can lead to excessively lush growth, which makes your plants more vulnerable to attack by pests (see Plant Profiles, pages 55–112, for greater detail on feeding).

Supporting your plants

As your plants grow bigger and bear fruit, they may require support to protect them from damage. When growing in containers, I prefer to choose dwarf varieties of the larger fruits and vegetables, as they tend to need less support. If your plants are doing well, however, you may need to ensure that they have something to lean on or climb up while they grow.

First off, it is fundamental to ensure that your plant is in a pot large enough to accommodate its full size. Not only will a plant in too small a pot run out of nutrients faster and need more frequent watering, but it may will become top-heavy and liable to topple over or snap.

Depending on the size of the fruit on the variety you're growing, tomatoes, peppers, and chilies may need staking to ensure their branches don't break as the fruit swells. Drive a bamboo cane into the soil 1in from the main stem and tie loosely to the stem with a natural twine, like jute. Keep an eye on it as the plant grows, and loosen the ties if the twine begins to cut into the widening stem.

Beans and peas may benefit from having something to scramble up as they put their tendrils out and climb towards the sky. Netting, canes, or even knobbly twigs can provide what they need to hold on to as they grow.

CAPSICUM ANNUUM
"PRETTY IN PURPLE"

Protecting your plants from pests

Container-grown plants can fall victim to pests, just as those growing in the ground can. However, since plants in pots generally need your attention more often, you're likely to spot any problems early enough to try and fix them.

Raising strong plants is the best first line of defense against any pest attack. In addition, consider encouraging a balanced ecosystem by creating an inviting environment for a pest's predators—such as ladybirds and their larvae, which love to eat aphids. Grow pollen- and nectar-rich flowers and create a habitat for beneficial insects (and eliminate the places where pests like to hide). Since I prefer to grow without chemicals, I try to accept that some pests are inevitable and are a valuable food source for many other creatures.

The list of potential pests is a long one, but below are the ones most likely to damage your edible plants and eat your harvest before you do if they get the chance:

Birds
Pigeons love to peck at your leafy plants and strip your brassicas, while garden birds such as blackbirds and sparrows love red fruit so will eat your ripe tomatoes. Installing nets draped over a frame, or a cage, can keep those little beaks from pecking holes in your precious crops. Also, old CDs (or a mirror ball!) hung on string near your crops will reflect the sunlight and should scare off pesky birds.

Slugs and snails
These slimy customers are every gardener's nemesis. They love feasting on young plants and new growth, but will munch on all kinds of plant matter. Filling a dish with a solution made from instant yeast or beer, sugar, and water will entice these pests into the liquid where they drown—it's a bit cruel, but it does work. You can also go out in the dark with a flashlight and pick them off, one by one. This approach can also be used to remove caterpillars, larvae, or egg sacs, and is a fairly manageable technique in a small growing space.

Sap-sucking insects
Aphids, whitefly, or thrips insert their mouthparts into plant tissue and drink the sugary sap inside. This causes stunted and deformed growth and can lead to the death of a plant. To deal with these pests, you can make a homemade garlic spray by steeping a few cloves in hot water overnight, straining, and diluting with more water. Spray directly onto the infested area of the plant.

Flying insects
These include fleas and are harder to control, but using insect-proof mesh is a good way to prevent damage to your plants.

Troubleshooting: diseases and nutrient deficiencies

As with pests, the list of diseases that a plant can fall victim to is a long one, and container-grown plants can be more vulnerable because stressed plants (from inadequate watering, for example) are easier targets. Prevention is always preferable to cure, so maintain good gardening hygiene by using clean pots and tools, resist the temptation to over-fertilize, and refrain from growing plants too close together, since good air flow is essential for plant health.

Diseases

Wilt is a bacterial disease that attacks plant tissue, damaging its water-transportation system and causing it to wilt. The plant will die if the disease is allowed to spread, so prune out affected leaves with a clean pair of scissors or snips and dispose of them away from your other plants.

Blight is a devastating disease that affects potatoes and tomatoes and causes the loss of chlorophyll, leading to the browning of the plant's tissues. It can cause the plant to die in a matter of days. To prevent it, avoid getting water on the plant's leaves. As with wilt, remove any diseased material and destroy it, preferably by burning or binning, to avoid the spores spreading farther.

Powdery mildew is a fungal disease that affects plants by coating them with a dust-like substance. It is rarely fatal but can stress the plant, making it less productive and more vulnerable to other pests and diseases. If spotted early, it can be treated with a solution of one part milk and three parts water sprayed all over the leaves while in the bright sun. Although it can affect a wide range of plants, the disease on one plant is unlikely to spread to a plant from a different family.

Downy mildew is a disease that thrives in wet conditions and causes discoloration of the top of leaves and mold growth underneath. To prevent it spreading, water your plants directly on the soil in the morning and avoid getting water on the leaves.

Rust is another fungal disease that mainly affects leaves and is identifiable by the distinctive rust-colored spots it causes. Remove and destroy the infected leaves as they appear in order to slow down the spread of the disease.

Gray mold can cause decay. Try to avoid overcrowding your plants, as the fungus can spread to a wide range of plants and there's no organic way to treat it.

Mosaic virus is a disease that also affects many plants, including tomatoes and zucchinis. The virus causes leaves to develop yellow and white spots and streaks, hence its name, and leads to stunted and deformed growth. This disease cannot be cured, so diseased plants should be removed and destroyed. Since it hides in many places and is spread by many pests, practising good gardening hygiene is essential.

Nutrient deficiencies

Nitrogen deficiency shows up as the yellowing of leaves and can be addressed by feeding regularly with nettle tea.

Phosphorus deficiency makes plants turn purplish on older leaves first and can be remedied with a well-rounded fertilizer such as comfrey tea or seaweed feed.

Potassium deficiency causes leaves to look yellow, scorched, and bronzed and begin to curl. Seaweed feed is rich in potassium, so its regular use will address this deficiency.

Blossom end rot is caused by inadequate levels of calcium and leads to the fruits developing a dark patch at the tip, where the flower was. It's more likely to be caused by irregular watering than lack of calcium in the compost, so keep your compost well watered.

CUCURBITA PEPO VAR.
CYLINDRICA "BURPEES
GOLDEN ZUCCHINI"

Small-scale composting with worms

Worms are an important decomposer—turning plant matter into nutritious worm poop—and you can harness this quality to make your own compost in a small space. Wormeries are ideal for creating compost from kitchen scraps and peelings. You can buy a ready-to-use "worm hotel," but it is straightforward to make a wormery from recycled materials.

The worms that are used in composting systems are not the same as the common earthworm. They are called brandling worms (also red or tiger worms) and live in decaying organic matter. You can find them in an existing compost heap, buy them online, or, even better, take some from another healthy wormery.

Building a wormery

A wormery made from three stacked boxes is simple to construct at home and easy to monitor and manage. The finished compost ends up in the bottom compartment, from where it can be removed without disturbing the worms and the emptied box returned to the top.

1 Get hold of three equal-sized containers (polystyrene boxes, plastic crates, old tins). I find local stores and cafés are great for finding sturdy containers that can be recycled.

2 For a container about the size of an old wine box, you'll need to drill or poke 12 holes in the bottom of each box, at least ¼in in diameter. These will allow the worms to move up through the levels, and water to drain out.

3 Put some bedding material, such as

newspaper, in the bottom box, and add the worms.

4 Add an inch or two of food waste; this should be enough to feed the worms for the first week, while they get used to their new home.

5 Stack the remaining boxes on top of the worm hotel, which should be lifted up on two bricks to help excess liquid drain away. Even better, put a tray underneath so that you can collect the liquid and use it as plant food.

6 Add food waste to the bottom container, gradually at first but increasing as your worm population grows. Once the bottom tray is full, start adding food waste to the tray above. The worms will migrate upwards to find the new food, leaving the compost behind ready to be harvested.

Feeding your wormery

Most food waste that can decompose can be added to a wormery, including:
- Raw and cooked fruits and vegetables
- Tea bags and coffee grounds
- Eggshells
- Small amounts of bread
- Shredded newspaper and card

Avoid adding:
- Citrus peel and alliums (such as onions and garlic), because worms prefer a neutral pH and these can make your wormery too acidic
- Meat, fish, and dairy because, although they can be decomposed by worms, they can also introduce bacteria into the compost and attract pests or rodents

Add food scraps in moderation to avoid overwhelming the worms: they are more likely to be killed by overfeeding than by starvation.

Worms are most active in warm, moist conditions, so be aware of temperature. Their activity declines below 50°F and above 85°F. Set up your wormery in the late spring or early summer and keep it sheltered—somewhere that doesn't get too cold or too warm. If the temperature does drop, you might need to give your worms some insulation by repurposing some bubble wrap, a piece of carpet, or an old blanket.

Nurturing your wormery

A wormery that's working well should not smell because the worms will be consuming the rotting material. Add more food waste only when the last batch has been largely processed to avoid the contents rotting, which your worms won't like and neither will you!

Make sure that what you add to the wormery is three-quarters plant material and one-quarter torn-up cardboard and newspaper to keep the environment balanced (add extra shredded newspaper if the contents of the wormery appear too wet).

What a wormery produces and how to use it

When worms eat and digest your kitchen scraps they produce nutrient-dense poop that you can use to feed your plants. This vermicompost can be applied to growing beds as a light top dressing for heavy feeders such as tomatoes, zucchinis, or potatoes.

It is also possible to soak the worm casts in water for a day and produce a "tea" that, when used to water plants, gives a dose of nutrients that the plants can take up quickly.

If you find that there are still worms in your finished compost, gather the compost by moving it all to one side of the container and then add new bedding and fresh food scraps to the empty side. After a week or so, the worms should have made their way over, leaving their casts behind for you to remove.

DON'T FORGET: your worms are living creatures in your care, and it's your responsibility to understand what they need to survive and thrive. If you're interested in learning more, The Urban Worm is a really helpful resource: theurbanworm.co.uk/faqs. There's a focus on soil regeneration and how-to guides for different containers and systems.

PLANT
PROFILES

Salad leaves

The first plants I learned to grow from seed were salad leaves. They're quite straightforward and you'll quickly find yourself harvesting leaves. Once you understand how to grow a lettuce, you'll be able to try your hand at chard, kale, arugula, sorrel, mustard leaves, and much more. So they're a good place to start your edible growing journey!

Timing

Summer lettuce seeds can be sown from early spring and transplanted into a larger container when they're big enough (6–8 weeks later). If they're going to be living outside, wait until the cold weather has passed before exposing them to life outdoors. Winter lettuces (such as endives and radicchio) can be sown from mid- to late summer for a harvest before the cold weather sets in, and can overwinter ready for an early harvest the following spring.

All salad leaves can be grown in trays indoors if you can provide enough light. I think plants grown indoors are best eaten when they're younger, as baby leaves, so instead of hoping for many harvests, enjoy them while they're delicious and then start again with a new sowing.

Getting started

Lettuce seeds are tiny, so they require only a very light covering of soil when they're sown. Sow one seed per module, or if you're sowing into a tray, sow a row of seeds and, when the seedlings are about 2in tall, remove the weakest ones (and eat them!) until you're left with a row of plants about 4in apart. Alternatively, transplant your seedlings into a larger container so that they have room to fill out. Providing the right amount of space makes harvesting easier. In addition, if there's a problem with one of your plants, you'll be able to remove it without disturbing the others.

Growing

Container

Lettuces have quite small root systems, so they can live in a pot or tray that's just 3in deep.

Water

Lettuces do require regular watering: a generous drink at least once a week and every few days in the hotter months. Allowing your plants to dry out during hot weather will stress them and may cause them to "bolt," or rush to push out flowers in an attempt to produce seed, because they believe they're about to die.

Light

As do most plants, lettuces appreciate a sunny spot. They don't like very hot sun, though, so be careful at the height of summer and on extremely sunny windowsills, and be ready to provide some shade if necessary.

Feeding

If your plants look as though they'd appreciate a boost of energy, feed them with nettle feed or liquid seaweed feed, both of which are high in the nitrogen that leafy plants need to thrive.

Harvesting

Pick the large outer leaves—with a swift and clean snap—leaving intact the growing heart at the center of the plant and a few surrounding leaves. In a week or two, your plant will be ready for harvesting again.

LACTUCA SATIVA
"BATAVIAN, TARENGO"
"COS, PARIS ISLAND"
"RED SALAD BOWL"
"COS, PARIS ISLAND"

Other plants to grow as salad leaves

Salad leaves can be grown for most of the year, and different varieties thrive at different times. With a little planning, you can have a regular supply of leaves with all manner of flavors, textures, and colors that will far outshine the average grocery store iceberg.

Chard

This member of the beet family has the capacity to grow enormous leaves that must be cooked before they are eaten, but when the plants are grown in a cluster, the leaves can be harvested young and provide a tasty and brightly coloured addition to your salad. Try growing the varieties "Rhubarb," "Canary" or "Five Colors."

Endive

A great addition to your winter salad mix, endives can withstand lower temperatures than many other salads. Their slightly bitter flavor isn't to everyone's taste, but they do offer welcome freshness at a time when the tender summer lettuces aren't around.

Mustards

This group of plants produce the most beautiful leaves, in vibrant greens and deep purples, and have a seriously punchy flavor. My favorites are "Scarlet Frills," "Green in Snow", and "Purple Wave." As a member of the brassica family, mustards grow well in cool weather and can be overwintered alongside your winter salad.

Kale

Although fully grown kale eaten raw can be a little tough on the digestive system, harvesting the leaves while they're small is both delicious and altogether easier on the stomach. Try growing the "Red Russian" variety or Cavolo Nero, both of which are great additions to your overwintering winter salad gang.

Arugula

This is a peppery option for your salad mix. As with the mustards, the younger leaves taste milder than the older ones. Arugula grows quite fast, and if it does bolt, the flowers are delicious as well as very pretty.

LACTUCA SATIVA
"BATAVIAN, TARENGO"
BETA VULGARIS SUBSP.
VULGARIS "RAINBOW CHARD"

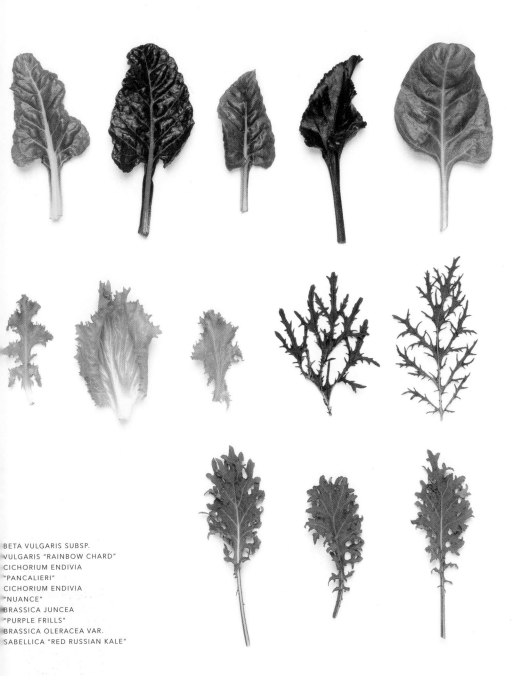

BETA VULGARIS SUBSP.
VULGARIS "RAINBOW CHARD"
CICHORIUM ENDIVIA
"PANCALIERI"
CICHORIUM ENDIVIA
"NUANCE"
BRASSICA JUNCEA
"PURPLE FRILLS"
BRASSICA OLERACEA VAR.
SABELLICA "RED RUSSIAN KALE"

Chilies and peppers

Chilies do well in containers and are great for growing indoors on a sunny windowsill, because they need warmth to thrive. Many varieties grow as compact plants, and the chilies themselves can be so pretty that it's as close to an ornamental plant as an edible plant can be. Just like their spicier brethren, peppers need warmth and lots of light to thrive. As warm-season plants, they need to be sheltered from cold weather, which can affect their growth, and from wind, which can snap their stems.

CAPSICUM ANNUUM
"SEMAROH EARLY"
"REDSKIN PATIO PLANT"

Timing
Chilies need the whole of the growing season to reach maturity, so the seeds should be sown early. They must be kept above 70°F if they are to germinate, so they're best started on a heat mat, in a heated propagator or warm airing cupboard.

Getting started
Sow chili seeds from late winter into early spring. The seeds are fairly small, so sow them about ¼in deep in moist seed compost and don't be too generous when watering: you don't want them to rot before they've had a chance to start growing. Each variety of chili has its own germination time, and some can take a couple of weeks, so be patient, keep the compost moist, and wait a few weeks before you consider sowing more seeds. Starting chili and pepper plants early—when the days are still short and the light levels low—can cause your

seedlings to stretch toward the light that they are especially desperate for. If you don't have a bright, south-facing windowsill, the glow of a grow light might be what your plants need to stop them from becoming leggy. Plug plants are a good option if you struggle to get your chili seedlings off to a strong and healthy start.

Peppers tend to grow more vigorously than chilies, so they may need potting on into a bigger pot more swiftly to accommodate their expanding root system and tall stature. If the sunny spot you've earmarked for your peppers is on a veranda or balcony, move the plants into their final position only when the night-time temperature is reliably above 60°F.

Growing

Container
Chili plants come in many different sizes, and a fully grown compact chili plant can be happy in a 0.6-gallon pot while a larger variety might need as much as a 2-gallon pot. Add a handful or two of gravel to the bottom of the pot before filling it with compost, to help with drainage.

The full size of a pepper plant depends on the variety, but they are invariably larger than chilies and most types will need a 2-gallon pot at least.

Water
Chilies and peppers will appreciate a regular watering but will survive if they dry out for a few days. Be moderate when watering in cool weather, to avoid your plants sitting in soggy soil, but when the temperature rises, be generous with water. If you let your plants dry out too regularly, they may produce less fruit.

Light
Chilies and peppers need a lot of sunlight to grow and produce fruit and also, just as importantly, to ripen that fruit. Make sure the spot you choose for your chili plant gets 8 hours of warm sun a day—more if possible— and is sheltered from the wind.

Feeding
It's important to make sure your chili plants have enough sustenance when they are flowering and setting fruit. Diluted comfrey tea or liquid seaweed every 10–14 days will provide a balanced feed, but avoid nitrogen-rich feed such as nettle, which will encourage leafy growth at the cost of fruit development.

Pollination
Just like tomatoes, chili flowers must be pollinated if they are to produce fruit, and they too produce perfect flowers. If you don't want to leave it to chance, hand-pollinate by using a very small paintbrush to move the pollen from the stamen (the shorter parts surrounding the stigma) to the stigma (the longest protruding part in the very center of the flower). Misting also helps to raise the humidity, which will help the fruit to establish.

Support
Most compact chili plants won't need support, but if you find they're struggling to grow upright, tying the main stem to a small stick (a chopstick or kabob skewer will do) should be enough support.

Pepper plants can grow quite tall and should bear abundant fruit, and, since peppers can be quite heavy, it might be necessary to push a stake (such as a stick, bamboo cane, or wooden spoon) into the soil an inch or two from the main stem and gently tie the plant to it with twine. If you want to encourage bushier growth,

remove the growing tip so the plant branches more vigorously sideways.

up to you to decide if you prefer quantity or sweet taste.

Harvesting

Harvest your chilies as soon as they are ripe, as this will encourage the plant to produce more flowers and fruit. You can eat them fresh, or dry them and bring some much-needed spicy warmth to cold winters.

You can harvest peppers when they are green, but the taste is far sweeter if you wait until they are fully ripe—yellow, orange, or red, depending on the variety. And yes, that does mean that the green peppers you've been eating were simply not yet ripe! If you do leave the peppers to ripen on the plant, it will be discouraged from producing more flowers and then fruit, so it's

Overwintering

With enough light and protection from cold, it's possible to keep a chili plant alive through the winter to fruit again for a second year. If your chili plants lived outside over the summer, bring them inside and find a spot on a sunny windowsill. Remove all the fruit and prune the branches back until you're left with a 6in stem. The plant will need some moisture, but water it sparingly, only when the compost becomes dry. Any remaining leaves may drop, but this is a normal reaction to lower temperatures and lessening light; they will make a comeback in the spring.

CAPSICUM ANNUUM
"PYRAMID CLUSTER"
"PRETTY IN PURPLE"

Tomatoes

When it comes to growing your own, tomatoes are the classic plant to try your hand at. There is nothing quite like the taste of a freshly harvested tomato, and if all you've had access to so far is grocery store specimens, you may well have no idea how delicious tomatoes can be! Those in the store are grown not for taste but for uniformity and ease of transport, harvested too early, and ripened artificially. So, give a tomato plant some of your coveted growing space and discover how fabulous home-grown tomatoes are!

Timing

Tomatoes are warm-weather plants, so they're grown only during the sunniest months. They should not be planted out until after the last frost has passed, and they slow down in growth and ripening as the temperatures drop and days shorten in fall.

You can sow your seeds in late winter or early spring—between 6 and 8 weeks before the last frost. It is essential to get started early, since tomatoes need to spend as much of the season as possible basking in warm sun to reach maturity, flower, produce fruit, and ripen it. If sowing seeds this early isn't an option, buying plug plants (seedlings grown commercially in individual modules, with strong root systems and ready to transplant) will give you a better chance of success.

Getting started

Given how tall tomato plants can grow, it's surprising how tiny their seeds are. Sow one seed per module into moist seed compost, cover the seeds with a very thin layer of soil, and water in generously but carefully, so you don't wash the seeds away. Tomato seeds must be kept at around 70°F to germinate, so it's worth using a heated propagator if you start early.

When your seedlings have their first true leaves, upgrade their dwelling to a 3in pot with fresh compost to keep them happy while they continue growing. You can move them to a slightly larger pot again if they outgrow their container, but only when they're about 6in tall can they be moved into their forever home. (Most plants prefer to graduate into increasingly bigger pots where possible, rather than moving straight into a large one; this prevents their roots from being surrounded by too much water and therefore supports the development of a strong root system.) When your young plants are tall enough, they can be transplanted into their final container. Take the time to harden them off and bury them deep—at least to the bottom branches—so that they grow a strong root system. Every one of those little hairs on the stem has the potential to turn into a root.

Growing

Container

Different varieties need containers of different sizes, however, all but the smallest cultivars (which will be happy in a hanging basket) require a pot or growbag with a capacity of at least 4 gallons.

Water

Giving your tomatoes the right amount of water is crucial if they are to thrive and produce tasty fruit. Erratic watering can make your plants stressed and susceptible to pests and diseases, and can cause the fruit to split. Tomatoes do need a lot of water, but if they are overwatered the fruit will be less sweet, and if the plants are left sitting in excess water, their roots may rot. Ideally, the soil will be moist throughout so that all the roots have access to the hydration they need. Tomato plants prefer a big drink once or twice a week over a light sprinkling every day.

LYCOPERSICON LYCOPERSICUM
"HOUSE"

Light

Tomatoes need at least 8 hours of sunlight a day when they're growing, and that is non-negotiable! If your spot is shady or the sun is obstructed for part of the day, your tomatoes will struggle.

Feeding

Tomatoes are very hungry plants, and if they're going to live in a container, they will appreciate having some organic fertilizer—such as seaweed meal—incorporated into the compost. When you see the first flowers appear, feed with liquid seaweed feed, and continue to do so every 10-14 days to give your plants the nutrients and minerals (especially potassium for fruiting) they need to grow, flower, and fruit successfully. Make sure to water generously when feeding, too.

Pollination

Tomatoes will not produce fruit unless their flowers are pollinated. Fortunately, they produce perfect flowers (the botanical term for those with both pollen-producing and fruit-bearing components), so, although they can be pollinated successfully without the help of a pollinator, the presence of a bumblebee or a gentle breeze will be a better guarantee of success. If you want to be absolutely certain that you'll have fruit to harvest, give your plants a gentle shake when they're in flower, or, better still, hold a vibrating electric toothbrush gently behind the open flower so that the pollen transfers onto the stigma.

Harvesting

Tomatoes are ready to harvest when they have taken on their mature colour (yellow, orange, black, or green, as well as red, depending on the variety). They can also be picked while still a little green and ripened somewhere warm, out of direct sunlight—and in the company of a banana if they need some encouragement. This method is particularly helpful for ripening the final fruits at the end of the season, when they are unlikely to ripen naturally on the plant.

Types and varieties

There are two types of tomato: indeterminate or cordon tomatoes, which can both become very large plants and, when happy, can produce large amounts of fruit; and determinate or bush tomatoes, which are better suited to containers because they are smaller, do not need pruning or supporting, and are quicker to offer up their bounty. Dwarf varieties are even more compact, so they can thrive in surprisingly modest containers.

Some varieties to try:
· "Hundreds and Thousands"—a prolific cascading cherry tomato plant that will grow happily in a container
· "Losetto"—another cascading cherry tomato, perfect for hanging baskets
· "House Dwarf"—a short and sturdy variety of cherry tomato, bred to be grown in pots

LYCOPERSICON ESCULENTUM
'HUNDREDS AND THOUSANDS'

Eggplants

Eggplants, which are related to tomatoes, need bright sun and lots of warmth to grow well, so they can be a challenge in cooler temperate climates. It's definitely still possible to grow them in those areas, but they need a bright, sheltered spot—preferably a sun trap—to thrive. I find growing eggplants very tricky, but I love eating them so I'll keep trying! Compact varieties do well in containers, and they range from the traditional deep purple to striped, white, round, and long types that both look amazing and taste delicious.

SOLANUM MELONGENA
"PATIO BABY"

Timing

Much like those of the chili, eggplant seeds need to be sown as early in the year as possible to allow them a long period of growth. It can take up to six months from sowing eggplant seed to harvesting the crop, so it's best to sow seed in late winter.

Getting started

Eggplant seeds look very similar to those of tomatoes, and require the same approach. Place the pots or trays in a heated propagator, since eggplants will germinate only when the temperature is kept steadily above 60°F, ideally closer to 75°F. As with all warmth-loving plants that are sown early, you must ensure

they get as much light as possible so that they don't become weak and leggy from stretching towards the sun. Young plants will need to be protected from cold, and you won't be able to move them to their final position outside until the nights are consistently above 60°F, and preferably higher.

Buying eggplants as plug plants can be very helpful. Seedlings started off in the perfect growing conditions are much more likely to grow into plants that produce flowers and fruit successfully, and I've found meeting their needs early on a particular challenge when starting eggplants from seed at home.

Growing

Container

Even compact eggplants are quite sizeable, so you will need a 2-gallon container, or larger, to accommodate the substantial root system that will develop.

Water

Water regularly and generously, as eggplants like moist but not soaked compost. Be extra-generous in very hot weather, and try not to let your eggplants dry out completely.

Light

Eggplants need as much sunlight and warmth as you can provide. It may even be worth moving the container to keep it in sunlight over the course of the day, to catch as many rays as possible. This will give your eggplant the best chance of producing a crop.

Feeding

Like their cousins the tomatoes, eggplants are hungry plants and will need feeding while they are producing flowers and developing fruit. Diluted comfrey tea or liquid seaweed every 10–14 days will provide the balance of nutrients your plants need to keep growing.

Pollination

Eggplant flowers must be pollinated to produce fruit, and they need pollinators to do that job, so make sure that flying insects can visit the flowers. Misting the plants twice daily can help the flowers and fruit to establish; it also raises the humidity around the plant, which it will appreciate. If your eggplant is one that produces large fruit, allow only four or five to develop on each plant and remove any new blossoms that emerge after that. Smaller varieties can be allowed to produce up to twice that amount of fruit, but they will also benefit from being limited so that they can concentrate their energy on the eggplants that have appeared.

Protection

Protect your eggplants if an unseasonably chilly night is forecast by covering them with fleece, as they are particularly sensitive to drops in temperature.

Support

Eggplants are heavy fruit and, with luck, your plant will have a good number of them, so it may benefit from being tied to a stake for support and to prevent the branches from snapping.

Harvesting

Cut eggplant fruits at the stem, using a sharp knife or secateurs, when they've swelled to maturity (dependent on the variety you're growing) and the skin is smooth and glossy.

SOLANUM MELONGENA
"LISTADA DE GANDIA"
"PATIO BABY"

Peas

Growing up, I hated peas because they were either boiled into tastelessness or gray and mushy—but, as I discovered later, freshly picked peas eaten straight from the pod are utterly joyful. Dwarf varieties can grow very happily in pots because, unlike the full-size varieties, they don't need lots of space or much in the way of support. If you pot up a few plants in a group they can support one another as their tendrils reach out for something to hold on to. As well as garden (or shelling) peas, the pods of which aren't edible, you can also grow sugar snap peas or mangetout, where you can—the clue's in the French name—eat the entire thing. If you've got a sunny windowsill, you can grow pea shoots as a microgreen, as their first tender leaves are a delicious addition to a salad mix.

Timing
Peas are a cool-season crop, so you can sow them as early as late winter and they will thrive in the cool spring weather. In fact, they're one of the first harvests you can expect in the season.

Getting started
You can sow pea seeds in toilet-roll tubes filled with seed compost, because peas produce long roots that don't like being disturbed later on. Soak your pea seeds in damp kitchen paper or a dish towel for 24–48 hours before you plan to plant them to make sure you only use seeds

that have germinated. You may find that a tiny root has emerged when you take them out to plant them, so be careful not to damage it when you put them into the seed compost.

Peas can be planted in their final containers once they're about 4in tall. Make a deep but narrow hole slightly larger than the toilet roll-turned-seed pot. Carefully peel off the card (which should be soggy and easy to remove), and place your pea seedling into the hole.

You can also sow pea seeds directly into their final container, but make sure to protect them from greedy mice, which love to munch on a freshly sown seed. You can cover your seeds with fleece or put a spiky deterrent over them until they start to grow, like chicken wire or holly clippings. Alternatively, borrow a cat to chase them away!

Growing

Container
Peas need 0.4–0.6 gallons of compost per plant, so a 2-gallon container filled with multipurpose compost should accommodate three or four plants comfortably.

Water
Peas need watering regularly, especially when the flowers and pods are forming, to ensure that you get a generous harvest. Avoid overwatering when the weather is cool, since this can lead to root rot, but once things start to warm up, your plants will appreciate a good soaking once a week. As the summer sun starts appearing more regularly, you may have to water more often; a good rule of thumb is to check the compost every couple of days by sinking your finger into it, and be sure not to let it dry out completely.

PISUM SATIVUM
"KERMESSE EARLY DWARF PEA PETIT-POIS TYPE"
"SNOW PEA"

Light

Peas need a bright spot to grow in, so place your container somewhere sunny.

Feeding

Peas don't need as much feeding as other fruiting plants, but incorporating seaweed meal into the compost when planting them out will give them extra nutritional support.

Pollination

Peas are self-fertile, meaning they can pollinate themselves, although they are more likely to be successful if a helpful insect dislodges the pollen to make it happen.

Protection

Young plants might need protecting from birds, so look out for peck marks on the leaves and, if necessary, net your plants to keep them out of the reach of greedy beaks.

Harvesting

Pick garden peas when the pods are firm and fat by holding the stem with one hand and pulling off the pods with the other or using snips to avoid damaging the plant. Pick sugar snap peas when they look like a ready-to-harvest garden pea. Despite the fact that they look very similar, remember that you don't have to shell these peas—you can eat the pod and all. Mangetout can be picked sooner after flowering than shelling peas, ideally when the pods aren't thick and the peas inside are still very small.

Start by harvesting the bottommost fruit, and work your way upward. The more you pick, the more peas the plant will produce, so keep on top of it.

Beans

Beans share some of their growing needs with their fellow legumes, the peas. Yet, unlike their cold-weather cousins, they love warm weather and will grow at an astonishing speed when the conditions are just right. There are a number of different varieties of bean—string beans, broad beans, climbing beans—but dwarf French beans are ideal for container gardening because they grow in a bush, need very little support, and are quick to produce a dinner-ready harvest. They come in a multitude of wonderful types, some with beautiful purple, cream, or yellow pods, as well as the traditional green.

Timing
Start your bean seeds indoors from late spring, but be sure the last frost has passed before you expose them to the elements: this tender crop will not survive a cold night. Dwarf beans produce less fruit than the climbing varieties, so you might want to sow another round of seeds in midsummer for a second harvest.

Getting started
Sow bean seeds as you would peas (see page 72) because, just like peas, beans hate having their roots bothered and toilet-roll tubes are longer than the average seed tray is deep. As with peas, soaking your beans in damp kitchen paper or dish towels means that you'll only plant out seeds that have definitely germinated.

It is possible to start your seeds directly in containers outdoors when there are signs that summer is arriving. However, I prefer to start beans with some protection from mice, which love to eat newly sown beans as much as they do peas, and from slugs, which are especially interested in the tasty young plants.

Beans can be planted in their final container when the risk of night frost has passed. Choose a sheltered position for the container: being exposed to cold or wind will compromise the vitality of the plants. If an unexpectedly chilly night is forecast after you've planted them out, protect them by covering them with horticultural fleece or moving them inside overnight.

Growing

Container

Dwarf bush beans will grow happily as long as the container is at least 8in deep. You can fit two or three plants in a 1-gallon container.

Water

Beans need only moderate amounts of water until they start to develop flowers and fruits. After that, check the moisture level of the compost every other day and give them a drink if the top inch or so is dry. Beans don't handle droughts well, and prolonged periods without water will cause the flowers and fruits to drop off.

Light

Beans appreciate a bright spot, but they can tolerate a little shade.

Feeding

Feed suitable for tomatoes and peppers, such as liquid seaweed, will provide your bean plants with the sustenance they need after a month or two, when all the nutrients in the compost have been exhausted. Apply every couple of weeks, especially when the plants are flowering and fruiting.

Pollination

Beans, like peas and tomatoes, can self-pollinate but benefit from being visited by bees or gently shaken by humans to make sure the process works.

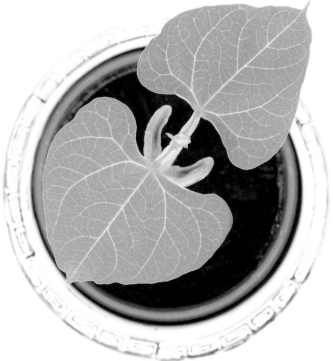

PHASEOLUS VULGARIS
"CONTENDER"

Harvesting

Beans are notoriously prolific producers of fruits, so get harvesting as soon as the pods are about 4in long. Keep picking, to encourage a more bountiful crop.

Towards the end of the season, you can leave the pods to grow larger and swell up, as the beans inside can be dried. At the end of the summer, cut the whole plant down and hang it by the stem somewhere sunny and dry. When the pods are crispy, shell the beans and store them for cooking during the winter.

PHASEOLUS VULGARIS
"CONTENDER"

Radishes

Radishes are one of the most satisfying crops to grow yourself, because many varieties transform from tiny seeds into crunchy, spicy little roots at lightning speed. Summer varieties take about a month to grow before you can harvest them, and they're small enough to grow in little pots tucked into a bright corner. Early sowings produce roots that are on the milder side, and the taste warms up as the weather does.

RAPHANUS SATIVUS
"SAXA"

Timing
Radishes are cool-season vegetables, so they can be started in early spring and sown all the way through until the end of summer. If the weather becomes very warm, however, they are prone to bolt and the root can become woody, so, unless you have a cool but bright spot for them, avoid sowing seeds during the warmest months. They will be ready to harvest 4–6 weeks after sowing.

Getting started
Sow radish seeds directly into the container they're going to live in, and keep them well-watered. Once the seedlings emerge, thin out the plants to 2in apart to give them space for the roots to swell.

RAPHANUS SATIVUS
"SAXA"
"FRENCH BREAKFAST"
"PEARL"
"PURPLE PLUM"

Growing

Container
Depending on the variety, radishes can grow in fairly small containers, needing a depth of no more than 6in. For longer varieties, such as "French Breakfast," a slightly deeper container is more suitable.

Water
Watering evenly is key to a successful crop, so make sure the compost is kept moist. Check the moisture level (by sticking your finger into the compost) to make sure you don't water already-wet compost, and don't leave your pots sitting in water otherwise the roots will rot.

Light
The plants must be in a spot that gets at least 8 hours of sunshine or the radishes will not develop properly.

Feeding
Radishes are such swift and unfussy crops that they'll be harvested and on your plate well before needing a feed to keep growing.

<u>Harvesting</u>

The best way to determine whether your radishes are ready to harvest is to give it a go. Keep a note of when you sowed the seed and, after 4 weeks have passed, pull one root up and see how it's doing. If it's well developed and tastes good, harvest the rest and enjoy them; if not, leave the rest to grow for a few more days. Timely harvesting is essential with radishes, though, and if you leave it even a few days too long the root will split and the taste will change—not for the better.

Potatoes

Growing your own potatoes is really straightforward. If you find the right sunny spot for them and give them plenty of water, they really can take care of themselves, although they will need a large container. There are many varieties, in all shapes, textures, colors, and tastes, but even the familiar types of potato are more delectable if you've grown them yourself.

Timing
Potatoes are divided into two main groups: earlies and maincrop. Early potatoes are quick to reach maturity and produce "new potatoes," whereas maincrop potatoes stay underground for longer and take up more space but will produce larger potatoes, some of which are ideal for storing. Early varieties lend themselves well to container growing, as the resulting plants are smaller than maincrops. Potato plants are started with seed potatoes, which are available to buy from midwinter and can be planted out during spring, depending on the variety.

Getting started
Seed potatoes look like potatoes that have been forgotten about in a cupboard and have started to sprout, but they're actually bred to be planted and yield healthy, disease-free potato plants. You can plant a sprouting potato from the grocery store, but you're not likely to get a good result, so it's worth getting your hands on proper seed potatoes from a reputable supplier.

The first thing to do is "chit" your seed potatoes—encourage them to start the growing process and develop sprouts before they are planted in compost. Place them with their sprouts (sometimes called eyes) facing upward in an egg carton or tray, and keep them somewhere light where the temperature doesn't drop below freezing. Your seed potatoes are ready to be planted when they've developed stout little shoots about 1in long.

Leaving all the sprouts to grow into stems will result in lots of very small potatoes, so rub off all but four sprouts before you plant the seed potatoes. Fill the container only one-third full with compost at this stage, and space the seed potatoes evenly, placing them sprout side up. Cover them entirely with 2in of compost. Check every few days and, as the leaves emerge from the compost, cover them with compost. This process, known as "earthing up," might seem counterintuitive but it sends a signal to the plant to develop more potatoes along the buried stem, so it will lead to a more impressive harvest. Make sure that any potatoes developing close to the surface of the compost are not exposed to sunlight, or they will start to turn green, rendering them unsuitable for eating.

Potato leaves are incredibly sensitive to cold, but earthing up before a forecast frost can protect the emerging leaves from damage. Alternatively, protect the young shoots by covering them with horticultural fleece, which is designed to shield plants from chilly weather. Or simply move the container to somewhere that won't get quite so cold.

Growing

Container
Potatoes need space to grow: each seed potato needs about 2 gallons of compost to call home, so when using an 8-gallon growbag, plant four seed potatoes, evenly spaced. A tall container will make the earthing-up process easier, but potatoes are fairly forgiving plants and can be grown in any large container that has adequate volume and drainage.

Water
Abundant watering is essential for potato plants to thrive, as they become large and very thirsty. When grown in containers, they will use up all the available moisture particularly quickly, so keep the watering regular so the soil doesn't dry out. Large containers will need a lot of water to make sure the entire root system gets a drink, so be generous.

SOLANUM TUBEROSUM
"CHARLOTTE"

Light

Potatoes grow best in ample sunshine, so make sure your container receives at least 6 hours a day. They can grow in light shade, but the yield will be smaller.

Feeding

Potatoes are hungry plants, so it's worth investing in compost designed for heavy feeders or adding a generous handful or two of seaweed meal to regular multipurpose compost before planting. A liquid feed of seaweed or comfrey every two weeks can be beneficial, but avoid nitrogen-rich feed such as nettle, as that will make the plants focus on leafy growth instead of developing potatoes.

<u>Harvesting</u>

Depending on the variety, your early potatoes will be ready to harvest between mid- to late summer, after the flowers have opened and are starting to fall off. How you harvest is up to you, and depends on how many potatoes you want to eat in one sitting! One way is to stick your hand into the compost and feel around until you have enough potatoes for your dinner. This method allows you to leave the remaining potatoes to grow on, especially if you can feel that they're not quite as big as you'd like. Alternatively, dump out the contents of the container and gather all your harvest at once—but make sure you eat early potatoes within a week or so of picking.

If you have grown a maincrop variety, wait until the foliage has begun to turn yellow and die back. Harvest the potatoes using the methods described above, but be sure to leave the potatoes to dry for a couple of days if you plan to store them. Store your potatoes somewhere dark and cool—inside a paper bag is ideal as any moisture will be able to escape.

SOLANUM TUBEROSUM
"CHARLOTTE"

Beets

As a child, I only ever tasted cooked grocery store beets. They were always a bit soggy and sour, and made all that they touched bright pink. Suffice to say, they were not my favorite. But as a grown-up vegetable fancier, I find my love for beets is constantly expanding. I've come to appreciate their earthy sweetness, and I adore the colours and tastes of the more unusual varieties, such as "Choggia," with its concentric circles of magenta and white, or golden beets, which are a bright, warm yellow in appearance and flavor. You can also eat the highly nutritious leaves, although take only a few at a time or your beets will stop growing.

Timing
You can sow beet seeds indoors from early spring, plant them out 4–6 weeks later, and harvest by early summer. Sow seeds every few weeks if you have the space, for a regular supply. Seeds sown in midsummer will yield roots that can be kept into winter, as long as they're harvested and stored before the first frost.

Getting started
Beet seeds benefit from being soaked before sowing, so put your seeds in a glass of water for 24 hours. Plant a couple of seeds in each module, as they grow well in a little group. Each seed is actually a cluster of seeds with the potential to produce a few germinated seedlings, so thin the bunch down to four or

five strong plants while they're still small. You can also sow directly into the final container. If you've used modules, transplant the seedlings while they've got two sets of leaves per plant: they won't appreciate being moved once they're bigger.

Growing

Container
Beets don't need a huge container, and you can plant one cluster of seedlings in a 1-gallon pot with a diameter of 9in. If you grow the plants close together, you will still get a harvest but the roots will be on the small side.

Water
It's important not to let your beet plants dry out or their roots will become woody, so be generous when you water, especially in hot, dry weather.

Light
Beets grow best in a sunny position, but they can tolerate some shade as long as they have had a strong start in life, with adequate light.

Feeding
Beets are vigorous growers and will benefit from feeding when grown in pots. A fortnightly feed of liquid seaweed or comfrey will support the plants to grow and roots to develop.

BETA VULGARIS
"BURPEES GOLDEN"
"CHOGGIA"

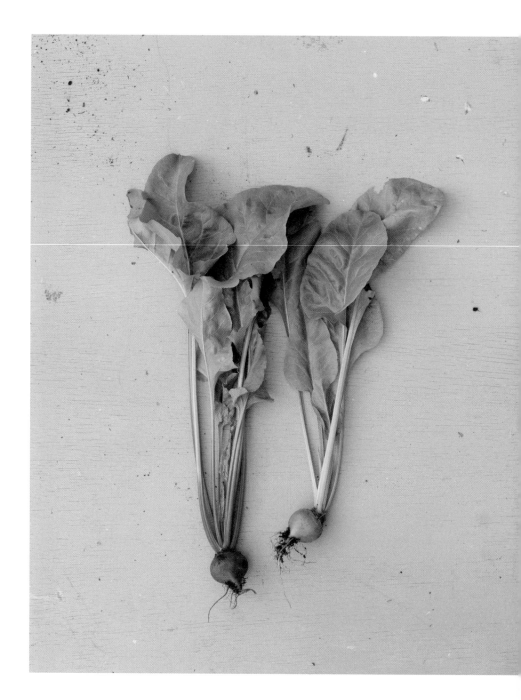

Harvesting

Your first beets harvest can arrive as early as two months after sowing, when the root is the size of a golf ball. At this stage you can also harvest the leaves and cook them as you would spinach. These early harvests will be the sweetest and most tender. Gently twist off the largest roots and leave the remaining ones to keep growing, harvesting them as you want to eat them. Just don't let them get much larger than a tennis ball, or they'll be tough and less delicious.

Zucchini

Zucchini is a space-hogging crop, but for all the room the plants take up, they pay you back with copious bounty. You need only one plant to produce as many as 30 fruits, so depending on how much you like the taste, one might be all you need. As well as regular-sized zucchini, you can harvest the flowers, the fruit when they're little, and—if you forget about them or are away for the weekend—enormous marrows! There are many varieties available, from green to yellow and stripy and in shapes that range from round to hook-necked.

Timing

Zucchini plants need sunny, warm weather to thrive, and they grow so quickly that there's little point starting them before the cold weather has well and truly passed. Seeds can be sown from late spring and planted out a few weeks later, after being hardened off, when the threat of frost is a distant memory.

Getting started

Sow one zucchini seed per small pot or large module. Place the seed on its side, pushing it down into the compost to double its depth.

Zucchini needs to be kept at about 55°F to germinate, so put the pots in a warm place and about a week later, when the seedlings emerge, keep them in a bright spot out of direct sunlight to grow on.

The young plants are ready to go into their final containers when they have two or three true leaves. Be careful to plant them at the same level in the soil, since burying the stem can cause it to rot. Keep an eye out for slugs, which like to munch on young zucchini plants.

Growing

Container

Zucchini are one of the biggest grow-your-own options, and even the bush varieties require at least a 6-gallon container, preferably 8-10 gallons if space allows. Those that are bred to be compact have a more upright habit, unlike the sprawling varieties that do better when grown in the ground.

Water

Zucchini in containers are very thirsty plants, so regular, thorough watering is important to support their vigorous growth, flowering, and fruiting. Aim your watering can at the compost surrounding the plant; avoid getting water on the leaves, as this can lead to fungal disease, and do not let it pool around the stem, which can lead to rotting.

Light

Zucchini plants need full sun and will grow most successfully with at least 8 hours of sunshine per day. They are best kept sheltered from wind.

Feeding

Like most fruiting plants, zucchini are ravenous feeders, so choose compost that is designed for such plants. You can also add a few generous handfuls of seaweed meal or garden compost to your container when preparing it for planting.

Once the plants are producing flowers and fruits, they will want a feed every 10–14 days with liquid seaweed or comfrey, which is high in the potassium and phosphorus they need to grow well.

Pollination

Zucchini plants produce separate fruit-bearing (traditionally referred to as female) flowers and pollen-producing (male) flowers on the same plant, and so require pollinators to visit both to ensure that the fruit-bearing flowers transform into fruit. Fruit-bearing flowers are identifiable by the bump at the base (which is the part that will swell into a zucchini); pollen-producing flowers grow with a straight stem. If there are enough pollinators flying around, successful pollination won't be a problem, but if you want to be sure of an abundant yield, you can hand-

CUCURBITA PEPO VAR. CYLINDRICA
"VERDE DI MILANO"

pollinate. Identify a pollen-producing flower and use a small paintbrush to gather pollen from the anther and transfer it to the stigma of fruit bearing flower.

<u>Harvesting</u>

You can harvest the pollen-producing flowers as soon as they're fully grown, but be careful not to cut off the fruit-bearing flowers by mistake, as that will mean no fruits! Also, make sure that you leave a couple of pollen-producing flowers for pollination. Zucchini flowers don't keep well, so refrigerate them as soon as possible and eat them within a couple of days.

When your zucchini appear, they will start coming fast, and keeping on top of harvesting will encourage the plant to keep producing.

When the zucchini are about 4in long and the flower has mostly died off, use a sharp knife to cut the fruit at the stem—and be careful, because the leaves can be a little spiky. Don't despair if you can't keep on top of the harvesting regularly, as even massive zucchini—also known as marrows—are delicious! And if you end up with more zucchini than you can handle—and yes, this does happen!—pick all the fruits you've got at once and share with your friends, family, and neighbors or, better still, make zucchini cake and share that too!

Annual herbs

PETROSELINUM CRISPUM
"PARSLEY, MOSS CURLED"
OCIMUM BASILICUM
"BASIL, GENOVESE"
OCIMUM BASILICUM
"BASIL, GREEK"

One of the most common reasons for people to say they're not green-fingered is because they think they've killed grocery store herbs—but I assure you, those herbs are not designed to survive! Much like salad leaves, annual herbs, such as parsley, cilantro, and basil, are fairly straightforward to grow from seed. If they're not trying to grow with their roots crowded into a tiny pot, like their store-bought brothers, they're more likely to survive to flavor more than one or two dishes. Some annual herbs come in wonderful varieties, such as Thai basil and cilantro "Confetti," that are far more interesting than the supermarket staples.

Timing
It's possible to grow annual herbs throughout the year. Parsley can be sown from early spring and grown for most of the year; it will slow down and even die back in the coldest months, only to return the following spring. Basil, on the other hand, needs warmth to germinate and grow. It can be sown from early spring on a heat mat or in a propagator, but you will need to wait another month or two to sow if you can't keep the sown seeds at 70°F. Cilantro can be sown from early in the summer months and will grow well into the winter; it must be kept well-watered while it is in active growth to avoid bolting.

Getting started
As with salad leaves, herbs can be started in trays indoors if there's enough light, and it's possible to grow a full herb plant on a bright, sunny windowsill. I like to sow 3–4 seeds in each module, as annual herbs grow well in small clusters and it makes harvesting quick and easy.

Growing

Container
Herbs don't need huge containers to grow in. I've planted three or four clusters of plants in a 0.2-gallon pot and they've grown quite happily.

Water
All the herbs mentioned above need regular watering, and you will have to increase it in hot weather. Basil plants are particularly susceptible to rot and mold, so don't let them sit in soggy soil and avoid splashing their leaves. Insufficient watering may cause your herbs to bolt or wilt, so try not to let the compost dry out completely.

Light
Herbs need a good dose of sunshine every day, so a bright windowsill is ideal. But they do need to be protected from very hot sun, so on those days you should relocate them temporarily.

Feeding
Because herb plants can be grown in relatively small pots for a while, they will need a nitrogen-rich feed to encourage more leafy growth when the compost nutrients are running low. Nettle or liquid seaweed every few weeks should do the trick.

Harvesting

Harvest parsley and cilantro with sharp scissors, cutting the tallest stalks and leaving intact the newly emerging leaves below. New growth will appear as long you don't cut all the leaves away at once.

Basil is best harvested by pinching off the tips of each stem, as this will encourage bushier, sideways growth and therefore more delicious leaves.

Perennial herbs

Unlike annual plants, which grow, produce seeds, and die in one growing season, perennials stay alive through more than two years of growing. Herbaceous perennial herbs, such as chives and mint, grow rapidly during the growing season but die back completely when the weather is cold, emerging again the following year. Woody perennial herbs— including rosemary, thyme, oregano, and sage— grow vigorously in spring and summer before becoming dormant during the winter. There are some fantastic varieties of perennial herbs, including lemon thyme, golden sage, chocolate mint, and garlic chives.

Getting started

Chives grow reliably from seed and can be started in spring, in the same way as annual herbs. The difference is that, instead of starting anew every year, your chive plants will effectively hibernate underground through the winter and start growing again in the spring.

Mint is one of the bullies of the plant world, and given half a chance it will spread into every corner it can find—so it is best confined to a pot. This aggressive growth habit makes it easy to propagate, and you can simply dig up and cut off a section of an existing plant and repot it in compost. As long as the new section has some roots, you'll have another vigorous plant in no time. If you'd like to see the process in action,

pop a mint cutting in a glass of water and watch the roots develop before potting up your new plants in compost.

Woody perennial herbs, such as thyme and rosemary, are not commonly started from seed, because germination can be slow and erratic and it takes a while for them to reach a point at which they can be harvested. It's best to propagate these types by taking cuttings or by division.

Take a softwood cutting in spring by using a sharp knife or pair of scissors and snipping off a 3in piece of young, new growth (it will be green and fleshy, not brown and woody). Remove the leaves from the bottom two-thirds and place the bare stem in a pot of multipurpose compost with a generous helping of vermiculite mixed in to aid drainage. Place the cutting somewhere bright but out of direct sunlight, and keep the compost moist.

The methods described above require access to a parent plant, of course. You're in luck if you have a friend or neighbor who is willing to let you take cuttings, but fortunately these herbs—in all their amazing varieties—can be found in garden centers and nurseries for much of the year.

If you buy a mature plant, it may have filled its container with roots and need repotting.

To do this, take the plant out of its pot, loosen the roots (this is especially important if they've grown into the shape of the pot), and plant in a larger container with fresh compost. You will then have your own parent plant to use if you want to increase your herb garden.

Rosemary, thyme, oregano, and sage are Mediterranean herbs, so they need really effective drainage. Add some gravel, grit, or sand to the compost in their new containers.

ALLIUM SCHOENOPRASUM
"CHIVES"
ORIGANUM VULGARE
VAR. HIRTUM
"OREGANO"

Growing

Container

Herbs can be grown in any container larger than 0.2 gallons, but it's worth upgrading to the next size up when the plant has filled the pot, especially if you notice its growth slowing down. Terra-cotta pots work well for Mediterranean herbs, as they prefer slightly drier conditions and water evaporates readily from this porous material.

Water

Chives and mint appreciate regular watering, whereas woody herbs need less and will complain if they are left in soggy, cold soil.

Light

All the herbs described above do best in full sun, but mint will tolerate some shade.

Feeding

As with annual herbs, your perennial plants might benefit from a nitrogen-rich feed to support their growth during spring and summer

Pruning

From the second year of growth, you can prune woody herbs in the spring once you can see clearly that they've started to grow. Cut back dead or damaged wood and trim the rest of the branches back to a pair of leaves, removing no more than a third of the plant. You can also do a light pruning after the plant has flowered over the summer.

SALVIA OFFICINALIS
"COMMON SAGE"

Harvesting

Use a sharp pair of scissors to harvest the stems and leaves of all the herbs described above, snipping off the tender, flavorful tips. Chives can be cut all the way to the ground, as that's where they will grow back from.

THYMUS PULEGIOIDES
"BROAD-LEAVED THYME"
SALVIA OFFICINALIS
"PURPLE SAGE"
ORIGANUM MAJORANA
"MARJORAM"
THYMUS VULGARIS
"COMMON THYME"
MENTHA X PIPERITA
"PEPPERMINT"

Edible flowers

Although my true love is growing vegetables, I also enjoy and appreciate the skill that goes into cultivating ornamental plants that are grown principally for their beauty and scent. Luckily, there are plants that are a feast both for the eyes and for the palate, and that are perfect for containers. Nasturtiums, violas, and calendula (marigolds) are easy to grow, and bloom in the most vibrant colors. These beautiful, delicious, and nutritious flowers can be sprinkled over a salad, used to decorate cakes, or frozen into ice cubes to adorn summer cocktails.

Timing
These edible flowers start growing in the spring and flower from early summer until cold weather stops them in their tracks. As a lover of cool weather, violas can also be sown in early fall and may flower all year long if the winter is mild, or if they have some protection from the cold and the wind.

Getting started
Nasturtiums, violas, and calendula can all be started indoors in late winter or early spring, their seeds sown in modules for transplanting into their final containers after the nights are no longer freezing. As with annual herbs, you can sow a few seeds per module so that the seedlings come up in small clusters.

It's also possible to sow seeds directly from late spring, straight into a pot full of compost where the plants will live their whole lives. Calendula especially do well when sown direct, so scatter a generous number of seeds and remove the least vigorous plants if they all germinate and the pot becomes crowded.

Growing

Container
As with annual herbs, you can grow edible flowers in fairly small containers. A 0.2- or 0.4-gallon pot has enough space for 3 or 4 clusters of plants, but if you find they're growing really well, you can remove a couple of the smaller plants to make space for the larger ones.

Water
For your edible flower plants to flourish and bloom, regular watering is essential. A good soaking once a week at least—and more often in the summer—will do the trick.

Light
Edible flowers do best in a sunny spot, although both calendulas and nasturtiums can put up with a little shade if necessary. Violas don't like it too hot, so choose a spot that's bright but a little cool, if possible.

Feeding
Generally, these edible flowers will do just fine growing in multipurpose compost without being fed—especially nasturtiums, which thrive in low-nutrient growing mediums, as in nutrient-rich compost they will produce more leaves and fewer flowers. Violas and calendulas can be supported with a weak liquid feed of seaweed or comfrey every couple of weeks, particularly when they're in flower.

CALENDULA OFFICINALIS
"CALENDULA"
VIOLA TRICOLOR
"VIOLA"
TROPAEOLUM MAJUS
"NASTURTIUM"

Harvesting

Pick edible flowers as early in the morning as possible, before they've seen too much sun, as that is when they will be most flavorsome. Wash them by dipping the blooms in water and gently shake them to get rid of any insects that might have clung to the petals.

These flowers are best when eaten as soon as possible, but if that's not practical, you can store them in the fridge for a short time. Place them in a single layer in a shallow container, covered with a dry paper towel, and eat within a day or two.

Microgreens

Microgreens are proof that, no matter how little space you have, anyone can grow something for their dinner plate. Microgreens are young plants that are harvested when they're between 1 and 2in tall, either when the first seed leaves have unfurled or when the next "true leaves" have emerged. These nutrient-dense little leaves are quick and easy to cultivate and a great option for those with very little sunny space to grow plants. With just a small seed tray, a little compost, seeds, and a bright windowsill, you could be harvesting your own microgreens within a month! All plants that produce edible leaves can be grown as microgreens, and basil, dillweed, radish, mustard greens, cilantro, chard, broccoli, beets, arugula, and peas work particularly well.

Timing
Microgreens can be grown all year round. These little plants may struggle in the low light of winter, though, so to keep growing them throughout the colder months you might need to use a heat mat and grow light.

Getting started
Fill a seed tray two-thirds full of compost and level it. Sprinkle the seeds evenly over the compost, densely for smaller microgreens and more sparsely if you'd rather harvest larger seedlings. Cover the seeds either with a fine layer of compost or with a paper towel to

block out light while they germinate. Water the seed tray well using a watering can with a rose attached, and keep the compost moist until the plants start to grow. Carefully remove the paper towel, if used, once the leaves are visible, as they will then be ready to see sunlight.

Growing

Container
Since these little plants won't require space for a sizeable root system, they can be grown in a tray as shallow as 2in.

Water
Keeping your microgreens tray evenly and regularly watered is key for healthy growth, and sticking your finger down into the compost is the easiest way to tell if the seedlings need a drink. Underwatering can cause wilting, from which young plants are unlikely to recover,

and overwatering can drown them, so aim for even moisture at all times. Using a watering can with a rose ensures that you can water your seedlings without being too disruptive to their delicate leaves and roots. Pay extra attention if you are using a heat mat, as the compost is likely to dry out more quickly.

Light
Even brand-new seedlings need to photosynthesize so, once they've emerged, place the tray in a bright spot. Be sure not to leave them in very strong sunlight as they may get scorched.

Feeding
Your microgreens will be harvested and on your plate long before they need any supplementary nutrients, so there's no need to feed them.

OCIMUM BASILICUM
"PURPLE BASIL"
BRASSICA OLERACEA
VAR. SABELLICA
"RED RUSSIAN KALE"

<u>Harvesting</u>

Harvest your microgreens early or late in the day, when it is cool, so that they are less likely to wilt. Gather a loose handful of leaves and, using a very sharp pair of scissors, snip the stems ½in above the soil, gently shaking off any soil that has stuck to the stems. Give your microgreens a quick rinse if they need it and eat them immediately, or store them as you would edible flowers and eat within 2 or 3 days. Once you've enjoyed your micro-harvest, get some fresh compost and start your next round of seed sowing!

Mushrooms

Mushrooms are one of my favorite foods, and when I was learning about growing edible plants, I was determined to learn how fungi fit into the picture. Mushrooms occupy their own kingdom of biological classification and behave completely differently from plants, so cultivating them for eating requires a different approach. The mushrooms we buy in the store and cook to eat are only the fruiting part of a fungus and, until you grow your own, you may never have seen the rest of the organism.

Timing
As mushrooms can be cultivated indoors and without sunlight, they can be grown throughout the year.

Getting started
Mushrooms reproduce by producing spores, tiny microscopic cells that are capable of replicating and growing as long as they find themselves on an appropriate food source or "substrate." By introducing the spores of a mushroom to a substrate (such as sawdust, straw, wood, or spent coffee grounds), it is possible to cultivate a fungus system (or mycelium) capable of bearing edible mushrooms.

The easiest way to grow mushrooms is to start with a kit. Mushroom-growing kits contain the substrate for the fungi both to live in and to consume, which has been successfully occupied by mycelium and is ready to be "shocked." Shocking is the process by which a mycelium-populated substrate is exposed to a stimulus, such as light or water, that kickstarts its reproductive cycle and causes it to start fruiting. Simply cut a hole in the bag containing the substrate and submerge in water to let your mycelium know that it's time to start growing mushrooms. After a week or two, tiny mushrooms—or pins—will start to appear, and they will double in size every day until they're ready to harvest.

It is possible to go through the process of gathering spores, sterilizing the food source material, introducing the spores, and leaving the mycelium for a month or so to occupy the substrate, but letting a professional do this part for you is the most reliable way to get started.

Growing

Container
The substrate in growing kits arrives wrapped in plastic (in which you make a hole to allow the mushrooms to emerge) and with a container suitable for cultivation, so additional containers are not needed.

Water
Keep the substrate moist by misting it with water from a spray bottle at least twice a day. The mushrooms will not grow unless conditions are kept humid.

Light
Mushrooms do not photosynthesize, so they don't need sunlight to grow. That means you can place the substrate in a shady corner or even a dark cupboard and they will still grow well—although they may grow towards any available light.

Feeding
The mycelium is feeding off the substrate it has colonized, so additional feeding isn't necessary.

LEUROTUS OSTREATUS
"PEARL OYSTER MUSHROOM"

<u>Harvesting</u>

When mushrooms bear fruits this is described as a "flush," and each populated substrate can provide up to three flushes. Once the mushrooms have been doubling in size for five or six days and the edges of their caps are starting to turn up, it's time to harvest by cutting them off at the base with a sharp knife. Then start the process all over again to cultivate flush number two!

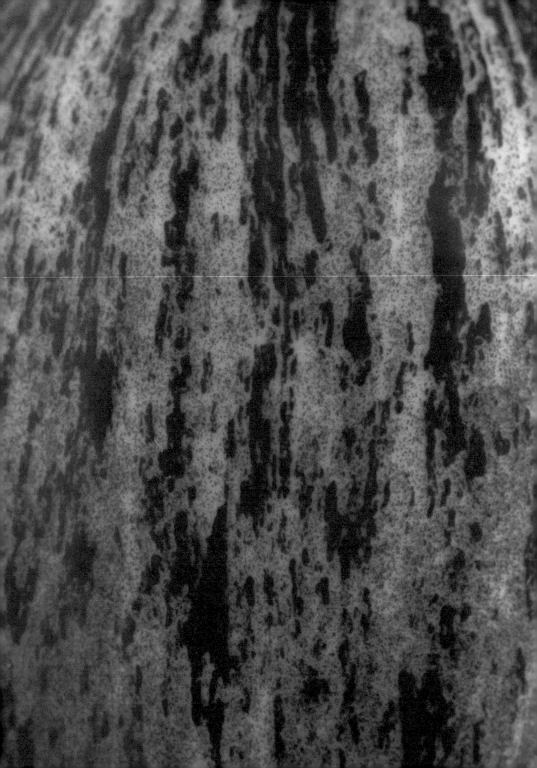

APPROACHES TO GROWING

Making the most of your small space

Gardeners with small spaces have to be innovative if they want to make the most of their containers. It helps to look at your space with fresh eyes and think about where you might be able to sneak in a few extra plants.

Grow vertically

Walls and fences can greatly increase your growing space if they are used well. Consider mounting small pots without drainage holes, into which smaller plastic pots of shallow-rooting crops such as herbs can be placed. Keep an eye on the watering: it's easy to leave a plant sitting in water or to forget about it completely when it lives higher up than eye level.

If your wall or fence is sunny, install a trellis and grow climbing varieties of plants such as French beans and zucchini, which will grow up towards the sun.

Hanging baskets

Although this will require a little more DIY confidence, it is quite straightforward to mount a wall bracket that's strong enough to hold a basket of tomato plants, lettuces, or herbs. This is a great option if your only outside space is on a veranda or by a door. Make sure you're drilling into a solid and stable wall, as it needs to be strong enough to support the weight of a hanging basket full of compost.

Create different levels

A good way of helping plants reach the sunlight they need to grow is to raise them off the ground, and it's only really possible when you're growing in containers. Using old furniture, boxes, and crates to raise pots off the ground and into the light will allow you to make the most of areas that are shaded at ground level.

Making the most of the season

When you have only a small space in which to grow edible plants, it's a good idea to make the most of the growing season by fitting in extra crops.

Successional sowing

With quick crops such as radishes or microgreens, it's possible to have a regular supply if you plan ahead. Instead of planting all your radish seeds together and harvesting them all at once a month or so later, plant a few seeds once a week for a steady supply. The same goes for lettuces: sow a few seeds at first and then, once their first outer leaves are ready to harvest, sow another round of seeds that will establish and grow while you're still enjoying your first plants. This is all about planning, so get out your growing diary and make a note of when you plan to sow each round of seeds.

Interplanting

If you have a large pot that is dedicated to a tomato or pepper, use the space around the base of the stem to sneak in a few small plants, such as lettuce or herbs. Basil is the perfect companion for a tomato, for example, because it deters certain pests that bother tomatoes, can be kept low and bushy with regular harvesting of the tips, and has a flavour that complements the fruit perfectly. Legend even has it that having basil nearby actually makes tomatoes taste better! Avoid putting two hungry plants in the same container, though, as they will compete for resources and neither will thrive.

Catch cropping

You'll find a point in the season when some of your precious growing space is empty. This is the perfect opportunity for a catch crop: a fast-growing plant that can fill the gap before your next crop is ready for planting. Radishes are ideal for filling holes in your growing calendar, or try herbs, chard, or kale grown as a microgreen or baby salad green.

Companion planting

Companion planting means growing plants side-by-side because they have characteristics that complement each other, perhaps to deter pests, enhance flavor, or encourage pollinators. It can increase the health and balance of the ecosystem in your growing space and it can add some welcome ornamental beauty to a space devoted mostly to edible plants. There's not always scientific proof to justify these pairings, but anecdotal evidence and the wisdom of many gardeners and growers are reason enough to give them a try!

Here are some popular companion plantings to try:

· Position chervil or cilantro next to plants that are suffering from aphid attack and they will deter the pests.
· The onion scent of chives keeps aphids away from tomatoes.
· Dillweed that has gone to flower will attract aphid-eating insects such as hoverflies and predatory wasps.
· French marigolds (Tagetes) grown near tomatoes deter whitefly.
· Calendula is a great companion for pest control as it attracts beneficial insects such as ladybugs, lacewings, and hoverflies that will also pollinate fruiting crops such as zucchini, peppers, and tomatoes.

· The strong scent of mint confuses and deters pests, including flea beetle, that chomp holes in brassica varieties (such as mustard greens and arugula).
· The fragrant and beautiful purple flowers of lavender attract a range of pollinators including bees and butterflies—and they can be made into a relaxing, and even sleep-inducing, tea.
· Thyme's strong scent is a deterrent for the black flies that may bother your bean plants, and if allowed to go to flower, is attractive to pollinators too.

When growing plants next to each other, it's still important to think of each plant's needs independently. If both plants do best in full sun, make sure the larger of the two doesn't cast shade on the smaller.

Saving seeds

Since the dawn of agriculture, people growing food have saved seeds from one season's crops to sow the following year. Yet with the advent of commercial seed production, this precious skill has declined, and most gardeners now buy seed. This has led to a steep drop in the diversity of varieties available to grow, and now saving seed is the only way that gardeners and growers can safeguard rare varieties for future generations. So, whether you want to replenish your seed stock in anticipation of next year's growing or are interested in preserving heritage varieties, saving seed is a wonderful and vital process.

Which seeds can be saved?

It is possible to save seed of all the plants featured in this book, but some are easier than others. It is easiest to save seed from plants that produce fruits—edible parts with visible seeds—and that produce perfect flowers that can self-pollinate. Tomatoes and peas are two such plants, and, since it is less likely that they will cross-pollinate, you stand a good chance of producing "true-to-type" plants from the seed you save. Avoiding cross-pollination is especially important if you're trying to save a heritage variety, because you need the seeds you save to be the offspring of two parents from the same variety.

The seeds of so-called F1 variety plants cannot be used to produce more of the same plant.

These varieties have been bred to express certain characteristics, but the breeding process means their offspring will never be "true to type," so saving their seeds is a waste of time.

The seed-saving process

If you have more than one plant to save seed from, choose the strongest, healthiest, and most delicious specimen. You want the next generation to have those traits, after all!

Peas produce dry seeds that are ready to collect when the seed pods ripen, indicated by a change of color from green to brown or black and the shell becoming dry. Collect pea seeds on a dry day when the ripened pod looks as though it's about to burst open.

Tomatoes produce wet seeds, which require fermenting to mimic the rotting that would occur in nature (or the effect of passing through an animal's digestive system):

1 Place the fleshy insides of a ripe tomato—which contain the seeds—in a jar and cover with water. Screw on the lid.

2 Leave the jar somewhere warm for three or four days, until the contents have developed a layer of mould.

3 Remove the rotten matter, add more water, and give the jar a vigorous shake.

4 Once the mixture has settled, the viable seeds will have sunk to the bottom and the useless seeds will float, so they're easy to get rid of. Repeat the shaking process a couple more times until only good seeds are left.

5 Place the viable seeds on a plate to dry out gently, away from strong sunlight and direct sources of heat.

Storage

Most seeds must be stored in cool, dry, dark conditions—the opposite of what is required for germination, in fact. Some seeds last longer than others, so maintaining ideal storage conditions can ensure a seed's optimal viability. Kept in these conditions, tomato seeds, for example, can last for up to 10 years and pea seeds up to 8 years.

First, throw away any seeds that appear damaged or not completely dried. Place viable seeds in labelled envelopes and keep them in a dry, airtight container, ideally somewhere that stays around 40°F (the refrigerator is perfect if other members of your family don't mind!). Excess moisture can lead to rotting, and

storing seeds with a desiccant such as silica gel (which can be bought online, but I save them from packets of ramen!) can help absorb any remaining moisture while they await sowing.

If you're interested in learning about saving seeds from plants that require extra steps for success, you can get more information and guidance from the Real Seed Catalogue (www.realseeds.co.uk) or Seed Savers (www.seedsavers.org).

Glossary

Annual A plant that goes through a full life cycle within one growing season. In areas with cold winters, this includes plants that would not survive freezing temperatures, such as tomatoes and eggplants.

Frost dates The timing of the last frost in spring and the first frost in late fall. Paying attention to when the temperature dips below 32°F is important for anyone growing edible plants, as the last frost determines when a plant can be moved outside and the first frost marks the end of the life of plants that won't survive the winter. It can be difficult to work out frost dates, and it's generally an estimation, so it's a good idea to chat to your gardening neighbors or friends and keep some fleece to hand.

Germination The point when a seed begins to transform into a plant.

Hardening off The gradual exposure of a plant to conditions outside. Your plants will be healthier and sturdier if you allow them time to acclimatize to life outdoors rather than giving them the shock of a sudden transition from a protected environment.

Overwintering Helping a plant to survive the winter. It is possible to overwinter a plant by providing it with protection or storing it until the warmer weather returns.

Perennial A plant that lives through more than two growing seasons and can survive a winter. Plants can do this by dying back so that the roots await the arrival of warmer weather to start growing again, by dropping all their leaves to wait out winter and growing them again in spring, or simply by ceasing to grow when temperatures are low. In warmer parts of the world, some perennial plants keep growing all year round.

Photosynthesis The process by which plants transform the energy of the sun into the energy they need to grow.

Pinching out Removing the growing tip of a plant to encourage side shoots to develop, leading to a more bushy plant.

Pollination The transfer of pollen from **stamen** to **stigma**, leading to fertilization and therefore the production of fruit and seeds.

Propagation The various ways that new plants can be made, including sowing seed, taking cuttings, dividing, and grafting.

Thinning out Removing excess seedlings or fruit to create space for the remaining ones to grow successfully.

Stamen The pollen-bearing (male) reproductive part of a plant.

Stigma The fruit-producing (female) reproductive part of a plant, which must be **pollinated** if fruit is to develop.

Variety A particular type of plant species. For example, a tomato (*Solanum lycopersicum*) is the species, and "Losetto" and "Purple Cherokee" are varieties of tomato.

Index

Acknowledgments

To Sam. This book is yours too. Thank you for your endless patience, love, and upholding. Thank you for putting up with the seedlings that grew on every available surface in our tiny flat and for your abundant energy—especially when mine was waning—while I was growing for and writing this book. I couldn't have done this without you and I wouldn't have wanted to.

To my Mum and Dad. I am deeply grateful for your belief in me and for your copious love and generosity. Your support never wavers even when I leap into the unfathomable and unknown. Thank you for always encouraging me to live a life of my own design. This book is for you.

To all my family, close and extended. Thank you for always cheering me on, keeping me positive and hopeful whenever I need it. To Daniel and Louise and to the Ayres, especially wonderful Pops—I hope my garden looks as lovely as yours if I make it to my 90s! To all my family in Mauritius and all the Ratinons and Ignaces around the world, everything I do is to make you proud.

To my friends, for celebrating my triumphs with me. To Emilie, Ann, Lucy, Alexis, and Rikki. And Fulya and Hasan, thank you for trusting me to grow plants in the garden of your café and to Sadie for lending me your tripod!

To my growing community for teaching me all that I know and for sharing the amazing adventure of the last few years with me. To Sophie, Hannah, Ximena, Sara, Alice, Jack, Beth, Becky, and all the green-fingered wonders who have shared their wisdom with me throughout the seasons.

Thank you to all the team at Laurence King, especially Zara for approaching me to write this book and for giving me the best birthday present in making it happen! And to Chelsea for being the most wonderful editor—thank you for guiding me through the process of creating a book. It's been a joy working with you.

Picture credits

All photographs were taken by Ida Riveros, Rita Platts, and Claire Ratinon except for page 6 which is by Andrew Montgomery/Immediate Media and the following images from Shutterstock.com:

Page 8: olpo; page 24: Ivan4es; page 30: Harry Wedzinga; page 38: Tom Gowanlock; page 54: logoboom; page 116: Tamara Kulikova.